TABITOMO Conversation with Pictures
「タビトモ会話」の使い方

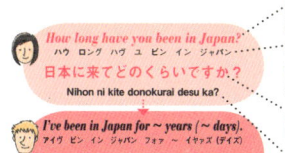

- **English** 英語
- **English pronunciation** 英語読み
- **Japanese** 日本語
- **Japanese pronunciation** 日本語読み

How long have you been in Japan?
ハウ ロング ハヴ ユ ビン イン ジャパン
日本に来てどのくらいですか？
Nihon ni kite donokurai desu ka?

I've been in Japan for ~ years (~ days).
アイヴ ビン イン ジャパン フォァ ~ イヤーズ (デイズ)
~年（~日）日本にいます。
~ nen(~ nichi) nihon ni imasu.

 Foreigners 外国人  Japanese 日本人

Foreigners are on the left, Japanese are on the right.
※外国人と日本人を示し分けています。左側の男女が外国人、右側の男女が日本人を表しています。

Illustrated words
大きなイラスト単語

Detailed expressions and words you can use with each phrase.

大イラストに描かれている個々の名称、想定される単語なども詳しく示しました。フレーズ例と組み合わせる単語としても使えます。

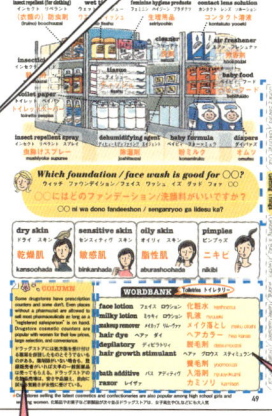

Activity index
行動別インデックス

Color tabs allow you to search by activity.

日本でしたいことを行動別に検索できるインデックスです。区切りをつけて色別に構成しました。

Wordbank
ワードバンク

Essential vocabulary for various situations

入れかえ単語以外で、場面で連想され

Notes
はみ出し情報

Tips and handy information

知っておくと便利な情報を1行でまとめました。

Columns
コラム

Useful advice on culture, manners, etc.

日本の文化、
スなど役立つ
めました。

Getting Started | Getting Out | Getting Things | Getting a Bite | Getting Along | Getting Understood | Getting Proficient

Table of Contents 目次

Getting Started はじめよう
Manga マンガ ... 4
- Introducing yourself 自己紹介・自分のことを話そう ... 6
- Greetings, thanks, apologies あいさつやお礼・おわび ... 8
- Speaking to people 話しかけよう ... 10
- Asking for information 教えてもらおう ... 12

Getting Out 歩こう
Manga マンガ ... 14
- Asking for directions 道を尋ねよう ... 16
- Riding buses and taxis バス・タクシーに乗ろう ... 18
- Riding trains 電車に乗ろう ... 20
- Riding cars and bicycles 自動車・自転車に乗ろう ... 22
- Signs around town 街で見かける標識 ... 24
- Staying at hotels and other facilities 宿泊施設に泊まろう ... 26
- Etiquette at Japanese-style inns 旅館のマナー・過ごし方 ... 28
- Visiting a hot spring spa 温泉に行こう ... 30
- Hot spring bath etiquette 温泉のマナー ... 32
- Enjoying recreational activities 余暇・娯楽を楽しもう ... 34

Getting Things 買おう
Manga マンガ ... 36
- Making full use of convenience stores コンビニを使いこなそう ... 38
- Using fleamarkets and thrift shops フリーマーケット・リサイクルショップを利用しよう ... 40
- Tokyo's specialized shopping districts 東京の専門店街 ... 42
- Shopping streets 商店街 ... 44
- Buying daily sundries 生活雑貨を買おう ... 46
- Drugstore ドラッグストア ... 48
- Electrical appliances and furniture 家電製品・家具 ... 50
- Being a smart shopper お得に買物しよう ... 52

Getting a Bite 食べよう
Manga マンガ ... 54
- Eating out 外食を楽しもう ... 56
- Restaurant talk 飲食店でのやり取り ... 58
- Conveyor belt sushi bar 回転寿司 ... 60
- Eating inexpensively お金をかけずに食べよう ... 62
- Going drinking 飲みに行こう ... 64

LIFE IN JAPAN
日本で暮らそう

英語 [English] + 日本語 [Japanese]

Getting Along 暮らそう

Manga マンガ ………………… 66

Housing 家を借りよう	68
Moving 引っ越し	70
Visiting a home 家を訪問しよう	72
Housework 家事	74
Cooking 料理	76
Socializing with neighbors 近所づきあい	78
Weddings and funerals 結婚式と葬式	80
Pregnancy and childbirth 妊娠と出産	82
Parenting 育児・子供と遊ぶ	84
Kindergarten/Nursery school 幼稚園・保育園	86
School 学校と行事	88
School life 学校生活	90
Company 会社	92
Workplace etiquette 職場のルールとマナー	94
Workplace talk 職場でのやり取り	96
Taking phone calls, office supplies 電話応対・事務用品	98
Bank, post office 銀行・郵便局	100
Government offices 役所	102
Seeing a doctor 診察の予約・健康診断	104
Beauty salon, barber shop 美容院・理髪店	106

Getting Understood 伝えよう

Manga マンガ ………………… 108

Time 時間	110
Numbers 数字	112
Year, month, date, day 年月日・曜日	114
Body, physical condition 体・体調	116
Illnesses, injuries 病気・けが	118
Worries 心配ごと	120
Accidents and problems 事故・トラブル	122
column Clothing/Shoes Conversion Table 衣服・靴のサイズ対照表	124

Getting Proficient 知っておこう

Facts & Figures 日本の基礎データと度量衡換算表	126
Learn more about Japan 日本にまつわる雑学ガイド	128
Useful expressions 簡単ひとことフレーズ講座	134
Vocabulary list アルファベット順日本語単語帳	136

Getting Started
はじめよう

Eye contact アイコンタクト

Japanese people don't usually smile at or talk to people they don't know.
日本人は、知らない人にほほえんだり、話しかけたりはあまりしない。

So a smile can lead to misunderstanding.
だから目が合ってほほえまれるとついかんちがい。

あら♥ 私に気があるのかしら？
I think he likes me!

ちがうよ…
Wrong.

ニコッ

But as women get older, they come to talk quite a lot.
ただ、おばちゃんになると、知らない人にもガンガン話しかけるようになります。

兄ちゃん、どこから来たんかいな
Where are you from, young man?

今日は暑いなあ
It sure is hot today!

僕!?

これ、何の行列？
What's this line for?

Festival lovers? お祭り好き？

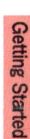

Japan has many seasonal events.
日本には季節のイベントが多い。

Lucky "setsubun" sushi roll*
節分の恵方巻き

Spring cherry blossom-viewing
春は桜の下で花見

Winter snow-viewing at hot spring baths
冬は雪見温泉

Festivals from other regions and countries are also incorporated.
Asakusa has a "Samba Carnival".
Originally a Kochi Prefecture festival dance, the YOSAKOI is now enjoyed by people in 60 areas nationwide!

ほかの国や地方のお祭りも取り入れる。
浅草ではサンバカーニバル。
高知県のよさこい踊りは全国に広がり、
今や60もの地域がYOSAKOIを踊りまくる！

よっちょれ
よっちょれ

Yocchore Yocchore

日本って楽しければ何でもアリなんですね！
In Japan, if it's fun, anything goes!

うまいものがあればよりヨシだニャー
And if there's some tasty food, that's even better.

日本人はみんなで集まって楽しみたいのよ。
Japanese people like to have fun in large groups.

オレも！
Me too!

ニャー
Meow!

*Eating a thick sushi roll on setsubun for good luck was originally an Osaka custom, but is now done all over the country.　節分に太巻き寿司を食べると縁起がいいという大阪を中心とした風習が、全国的に広がった

Introducing yourself

イントロデューィング ユアァセゥフ

自己紹介・自分のことを話そう

Jikoshookai, Jibun no koto o hanasoo

はじめよう / 歩こう / 買おう / 食べよう / 暮らそう / 伝えよう / 知っておこう

Nice to meet you. My name is ○○.
ナイス トゥ ミート ユ マイ ネイム イズ ○○
はじめまして。○○と申します
Hajimemashite. ○○ to mooshimasu.

What country are you from?
ワット カントリィ アァ ユ フロム
お国はどちらですか？
Okuni wa dochira desu ka?

I'm from ○○.
アイム フロム ○○
○○から来ました
○○ kara kimashita.

What kind of work do you do?
ワット カインド オヴ ワァク ドゥ ユ ドゥ
お仕事は何をなさっているんですか？
Oshigoto wa nani o nasatte irundesu ka?

I'm a teacher.
アイム ア ティーチャァ
教師です
Kyooshi desu.

I work for a ○○ company.
アイ ワーァク フォア ア ○○ カンパニィ
○○関係の会社に勤めています
○○ kankei no kaisha ni tsutomete imasu.

---

systems engineer
スィステム エンジニァァ
システムエンジニア
shisutemu enjinia

cook
クック
調理師
choorishi

construction
カンストラクシュン
建設
kensetsu

WORDBANK — Occupations 職業

English	カタカナ	漢字	romaji
driver	ドライヴァァ	運転手	untenshu
store clerk	ストァ クラーァク	店員	ten-in
construction worker	カンストラクシュン ワァカァ	土木作業員	doboku sagyooin
hairdresser	ヘアァドレッサァ	美容師	biyooshi
nurse	ナーァス	看護士	kangoshi
finance	ファイナンス	金融	kin-yuu
medical	メディカゥ	医療	iryoo
manufacturing	マニュファクチャリング	製造業	seizoogyoo
food	フード	食品	shokuhin

★Supermarkets, convenience stores, and restaurants often post help-wanted ads in their front windows.
スーパーやコンビニ、飲食店のアルバイトは、店頭の窓ガラスに募集広告が出ていることが多い

How long have you been in Japan?
ハウ ロング ハヴ ユ ビン イン ジャパン

日本に来てどのくらいですか？

Nihon ni kite donokurai desu ka?

COLUMN

Whereas people in the West usually do not specify whether a brother or sister is "older" or "younger," the Japanese words for "brother" and "sister" always make this distinction clear. Moreover, since polite language is used for superiors, you must note whether the person you are speaking to is older or younger than you.

欧米では兄弟姉妹が年上か年下かをあまり区別して言わないが、日本では、「兄」「弟」、「姉」「妹」のように区別し、呼び分けている。また、日本語では目上の人には丁寧語を使うので、相手が年上か年下かを気にする必要がある。

I've been in Japan for ~ years (~ days).
アイヴ ビン イン ジャパン フォア ～ イヤァズ (デイズ)

～年（～日）日本にいます

~ nen(~ nichi) nihon ni imasu.

I have two children.
アイ ハヴ トゥー チゥドレン

子供が2人います

Kodomo ga futari imasu.

I'm married.
アイム マリード

結婚しています

Kekkon shite imasu.

| family
ファムリィ

家族
kazoku | parents
ペアレンツ

両親
ryooshin | husband
ハズバンド

夫
otto | wife
ワイフ

妻
tsuma |

I'm a ○○ person.
アイム ア ○○ パァスン

私は○○な人なんです

Watashi wa ○○ na hito nandesu.

nice personality
ナイス パァスナリティィ

人柄がいい
hitogara ga ii

●**Personality** 性格

talkative
トーカティブ
おしゃべりな
oshaberi na

quiet
クワイエット
おとなしい
otonashii

cheerful
チアァフゥ
明るい
akarui

aggressive
アグレッスィヴ
積極的な
sekkyokuteki na

serious
スィアリアス
まじめな
majime na

easygoing
イーズィーゴウイング
のんびりした
nombiri shita

interesting
インタレスティング
面白い
omoshiroi

cautious
コーシャス
慎重な
shinchoo na

★Asking a person you've just met about their age or marital status is also considered improper in Japan.
日本でも、初対面で年齢や結婚しているかどうかなどをたずねるのはNG

Greetings, thanks, apologies

グリーティングズ サンクス アパロジィズ

あいさつや お礼・おわび
Aisatsu ya orei, owabi

 ·······▶ Casual expression. Used for close friends/relations.
カジュアルな表現。親しい人に対して使う

·······▶ Formal expression. Used for superiors.
フォーマルな表現。目上の人に対して使う

Good morning.
グッド モーァニング

おはよう

Ohayoo.

Good morning.
グッド モーァニング

おはようございます

Ohayoo gozaimasu.

Good day.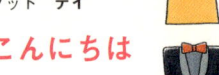
グッド デイ

こんにちは

Kon-nichiwa.

Good evening.
グッド イーヴニング

こんばんは

Kombanwa.

Good night.
グッド ナイト

おやすみなさい

Oyasuminasai.

See you.
スィー ユ

じゃあね

Jaane.

Goodbye.
グッドバイ

さようなら

Sayoonara.

Excuse me.
イクスキューズ ミ

失礼します

Shitsureishimasu.

Say hello to ○○.
セイ ヘロウ トゥ ○○

○○によろしくね

○○ ni yoroshiku ne.

Give my regards to ○○.
ギヴ マイ リガァズ トゥ ○○

○○さんによろしくお伝えください

○○san ni yoroshiku otsutae kudasai.

Long time no see.
ロング タイム ノウ スィー

久しぶり

Hisashiburi.

My apologies for not contacting you.
マイ アパロジィズ フォア ナット カンタクティング ユ

ごぶさたしております

Gobusata shiteorimasu.

🌸 COLUMN

Japanese has greetings such as "*itadakimasu*," "*gochisōsama*," "*tadaima*," "*okaerinasai*," and "*yoroshiku onegaishimasu*" that are not used in English-speaking cultures. The dictionary translations of such expressions do not always work, so you needn't go out of your way to say the English equivalents of these expressions.

日本語の「いただきます」「ごちそうさま」「ただいま」「お帰りなさい」「よろしくお願いします」など、英語圏文化にないあいさつがある。そのまま英語に置き換えて使うと違和感があることも。無理に英語で言う必要はない。

★The expressions separated by dotted lines have the same meaning. Use casual/formal expressions in accordance with the situation. 上記の点線で区切られた表現は同様の意味。カジュアル/フォーマルで使い分けよう

Thanks.	**Thank you.**	**You're welcome.**
サンクス	サンキュ	ユアァ ウェゥカム
ありがとう	ありがとうございます	どういたしまして
Arigatoo.	Arigatoo gozaimasu.	Dooitashimashite.

Sorry.	**I'm sorry.**	**Please accept my apologies.**
サリィ	アイム サリィ	プリーズ アクセプト マイ アパロジィズ
ごめんね	どうもすみません	申し訳ありません
Gomen ne.	Doomo sumimasen.	Mooshiwake arimasen.

That's OK.	**Don't worry about it.**
ザッツ オウケイ	ドウント ウォリィ アバウト イット
大丈夫だよ	気になさらないでください
Daijoobu dayo.	Ki ni nasaranaide kudasai.

● **Informal greetings** 気軽なあいさつ

What's up?
ワッツ アップ
最近どう？
Saikin doo?

I'm doing pretty good. How about you?
アイム ドゥイング プリティ グッド ハウ アバウト ユ
元気でやってるよ。そっちは？
Genki de yatteru yo. Socchiwa?

So-so.
ソウソウ
まあまあかな
Maamaa kana.

I gotta get going.
アイ ガッタ ゲット ゴウイング
そろそろ行かなきゃ
Sorosoro ikanakya.

Let's meet again!
レッツ ミート アゲン
また会おうね！
Mata aoo ne.

Take care.
テイク ケアァ
気を付けてね
Ki o tsukete ne.

★ Speaking to an elder as if he/she were your friend is called "*tameguchi o kiku*."
年上の人に対して、友達に対するように話すことを「タメ口をきく」と言う

Speaking to people
スピーキング トゥ ピープゥ
話しかけよう
Hanashikakeyoo

Excuse me.
イクスキューズ ミ
すみません
Sumimasen.

May I ask you a question?
メイ アイ アスク ユ ア クエスチョン↑
ちょっとお聞きしたいのですが
Chotto okiki shitai no desu ga.

Certainly. What is it?
サーァトゥンリィ ワット イズ イット
いいですよ。何ですか？
Iidesu yo. Nandesu ka?

Nice weather, isn't it?
ナイス ウェザァ イズント イット
いいお天気ですね
Ii otenki desu ne.

It looks like rain.
イット ルックス ライク レイン
雨が降りそうですね
Ame ga furisoo desu ne.

COLUMN

In places where there are distinct seasons and the weather is subject to frequent changes, commenting on the weather is a common form of greeting. In Japan, too, small talk begins with remarks about the weather. References to cherry blossoms, the rainy season, pollen, and other local topics are common.

四季があって天気の変わりやすい所では、天気の話があいさつ代わりになる。日本でもちょっとした会話は天気の話題で始まる。特に桜や梅雨、花粉の季節など、その地方の生活に関わる話題は多い。

WORDBANK — Weather 天候

warm	ウォーァム	暖かい	atatakai
cool	クーゥ	涼しい	suzushii
cold	コウゥド	寒い	samui
muggy	マギィ	蒸し暑い	mushiatsui
sunny	サニィ	晴れた	hareta
windy	ウィンディ	風が強い	kaze ga tsuyoi
snowy	スノウィ	雪の	yukino
stormy	ストーァミィ	嵐の	arashino
temperature	テンパラチャァ	気温	kion

weather forecast
ウェザァ フォァァキャスト
天気予報
tenki yohoo

alert
アラーァト

警報
keihoo

evacuation
イヴァキュエイション

避難
hinan

★Japanese find English difficult, and may even shy away from speaking altogether. Try to address people in Japanese. 英語が苦手で話しかけられると逃げ出してしまう日本人も。最初だけでもまず日本語で話しかけてみよう

May I ask you a favor?
メイ アイ アスク ユア フェイヴァァ↑

お願いがあるのですが
Onegai ga aru no desu ga.

Wait a moment, please.
ウェイト ア モゥメント プリーズ

ちょっと待ってください
Chotto matte kudasai.

COLUMN

Japanese people tend to hide their true feelings until they develop a close relationship with someone, choosing instead to accommodate their conversation partner's moods. Look for a topic likely to interest the other person, and say something you think he or she will find pleasing. Don't forget to respond humbly to compliments. Lightly deflect an unwelcome suggestion with a remark such as "That sounds nice. Let's do that some time."

日本人は、かなり親しい関係になるまでは、「本音」を隠して相手の調子に合わせ、相手の気分を損ねないように会話することが多い。まずは、相手の乗ってきそうな話題をふり、相手の喜びそうなことを言う。相手にほめられたら謙遜するのを忘れずに。相手が自分の意にそぐわない提案をしてきたら「いいですね、またそのうちに」などと言ってさらりとかわす。

Sure, no problem.
シュアァ ノウ プラブレム

大丈夫ですよ
Daijoobu desu yo.

I don't understand.
アイ ドゥント アンダァスタンド

よくわからないなあ
Yoku wakaranai naa.

WORDBANK Responses あいづち

Well, ...	ウェゥ	ええと…	Eeto...
That's true.	ザッツ トゥルー	そうだね	Sooda ne.
I see.	アイ スィー	なるほど	Naruhodo.
Exactly.	イグザクトリィ	そのとおり	Sono toori.
You're kidding!	ユア キディング	うっそー！	Ussoo!
Really?	リアリィ↑	ほんと？	Honto?
Wow!	ワウ	すごい！	Sugoi!
And then?	アンド ゼン↑	それで？	Sorede?
Did you know?	ディジュ ノウ↑	ねえ知ってる？	Nee shitteru?

●Honorifics 敬称

○○-chan
チャン
○○ちゃん
○○chan

○○-kun
クン
○○くん
○○kun

○○-san
サン
○○さん
○○san

○○-sama
サマ
○○様
○○sama

Honorifics vary in accordance with age and degree of intimacy. Generally, "chan" is used for girls and "kun" for boys, but as they get older, both males and females are addressed as "san." People who are on familiar terms often use "chan" for adult men and women, or "kun" for grown men. In some cases, "kun" is used, regardless of gender, for subordinates or students. "Sama" is a very polite form of address used for clients or in written communication.

敬称は年齢や親しさに応じて使い分ける。一般に、女の子には「～ちゃん」、男の子には「～くん」、成長すると男女ともに「～さん」を使う。大人でも親しい間柄では、男女ともに「～ちゃん」を使ったり、男性に対して「～くん」を使ったりすることがよくある。上司から部下、教師から生徒に対しては、男女問わずに「～くん」を使う場合もある。「～様」は非常に丁寧な呼び方で、客に対して、または書き言葉で使う。

★Watch out for information on heavy rain/snow and tsunami alerts. Transportation facilities are sometimes affected, too. 気象予報の、豪雨や豪雪・津波警報などに注意しよう。交通機関に影響が出ることもある

Asking for information

アスキング フォア インファメイション
教えてもらおう
Oshiete moraoo

はじめよう / 歩こう / 買おう / 食べよう / 暮らそう / 伝えよう / 知っておこう

Please tell me about ~.
プリーズ テウ ミ アバウト ～

~について教えてください
~ ni tsuite oshiete kudasai.

How do you say this in Japanese?
ハウ ドゥ ユ セイ ズィス イン ジャパニーズ

これは日本語で何と言うんですか？
Kore wa nihongo de nanto iundesu ka?

Do you speak English?
ドゥ ユ スピーク イングリッシュ↑

英語は話しますか？
Eigo wa hanashimasu ka?

Could you write that down here?
クジュ ライト ザット ダウン ヒアァ↑

ここに書いてもらえますか？
Koko ni kaite moraemasu ka?

What did you just say?
ワット ディジュ ジャスト セイ↑

今何とおっしゃいましたか？
Ima nanto osshaimashita ka?

Could you say that again, please?
クジュ セイ ザット アゲン プリーズ↑

もう一度言ってもらえますか？
Moo ichido itte moraemasu ka?

Will you be my friend?
ウィウ ユ ビ マイ フレンド↑

友達になってもらえますか？
Tomodachi ni natte moraemasu ka?

Whereabouts do you live?
ウェアァアバウツ ドゥ ユ リヴ

どのあたりに住んでいるんですか？
Dono atari ni sunde irundesu ka?

Could you tell me your phone number?
クジュ テウ ミ ユアァ フォウン ナンバァ↑

電話番号を教えてもらえますか？
Denwabangoo o oshiete moraemasu ka?

E-mail address
イーメイウ アドレス

メールアドレス
meeru adoresu

★If people are speaking too quickly for you to understand, try saying "*Moosukoshi yukkuri hanashite.*"
会話が速くて聞き取れなかったら、「もう少しゆっくり話して」と言おう

Is there a problem?
イズ ゼァァ ア プラブレム↑
何かお困りですか？
Nanika okomari desu ka?

Are you looking for something?
ア ユ ルッキング フォア サムスィング↑
何かお探しですか？
Nanika osagashi desu ka?

How do I do that?
ハウ ドゥ アイ ドゥ ザット
それはどうやってやればいいですか？
Sore wa dooyatte yareba iidesu ka?

What is this?
ワット イズ ズィス
これは何ですか？
Kore wa nandesu ka?

Could you tell me how to ~ ?
クジュ テゥ ミ ハウ トゥ ~↑
~のしかたを教えてもらえますか？
~ no shikata o oshiete moraemasu ka?

What kind of ~ ?
ワット カインド オヴ ~
どんな種類の~？
Don-na shurui no ~ ?

I'm looking for ○○.
アイム ルッキング フォア ○○
○○を探しています
○○ o sagashite imasu.

How ~ ?
ハウ ~
どのくらい~？
Donokurai ~ ?

Where?
ウェアァ
どこで？
Doko de?

How much?
ハウ マッチ
いくら？
Ikura?

How many ~ ?
ハウ メニィ ~
いくつ~？
Ikutsu ~ ?

Yes
イェス
はい
Hai.

No
ノウ
いいえ
Iie.

COLUMN

When making a polite request in Japanese, preface your request with an "I'm sorry" or "I'm sorry to cause trouble," even if you have no real reason to apologize. When introducing oneself or asking for cooperation, it is also common to use a self-deprecating expression such as "Please be generous towards my failings."

日本語では、丁寧にお願いするときには、本来謝るべき場面でなくとも「申し訳ありませんが」「ご迷惑をおかけしますが」のように前置きしくからお願いする。また、自己紹介や協力を仰ぐときなどには、「いたらないところがあるかと思いますが、よろしくお願いします」のようにへりくだって言うことが多い。

That's not possible.
ザッツ ナット パッスィブゥ
ムリですね
Muri desu ne.

★Men and women use the same expressions when speaking politely, but in casual conversation, they end their sentences differently. 日本語は、丁寧語では男女の表現に差がないが、カジュアルな会話では文末に違いが出る

Getting Out
歩こう

Manners マナー

Japanese people's manners have gotten worse in recent years.
近年、日本人のマナーは低下してきている。

Not giving up seats.
席を譲らない。

Getting drunk.
酔っ払い。

Talking on cell phones while riding bikes.
自転車で携帯電話。

Women putting on makeup on the train. Can't anything be done about it?
電車内でメイクしてる女性。なんとかならないものか…

Before you know it, people will be dyeing their hair on the train.
しまいには、泡で毛染めする人とか出てきたりして。

ありえないっつーの
I doubt it.

Asking for directions

アスキング フォア
ディレクションズ
道を尋ねよう
Michi o tazuneyoo

Is there a bank near here?
イズ ゼアァ ア バンク ニアァ ヒアァ↑
この近くに銀行はありますか？
Kono chikaku ni ginkoo wa arimasu ka?

There's one on the other side of this street.
ゼアァズ ワン オン ズィ アザァ サイド オヴ ズィス ストリート
この通りの向かい側にあります
Kono toori no mukaigawa ni arimasu.

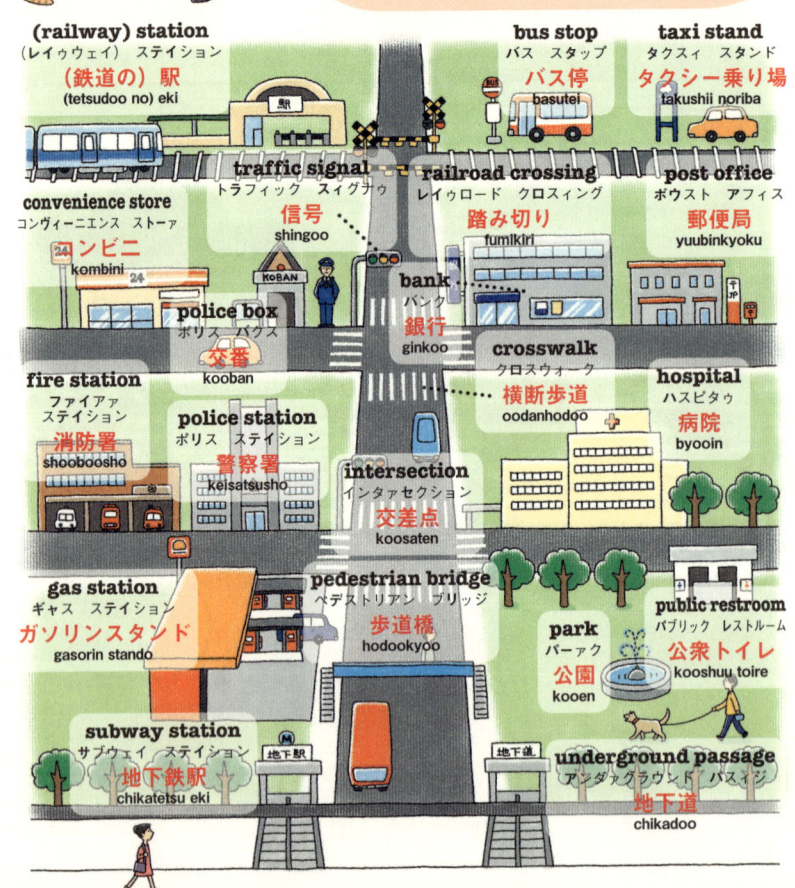

はじめよう | 歩こう | 買おう | 食べよう | 暮らそう | 伝えよう | 知っておこう

(railway) station (レイゥウェイ) ステイション
（鉄道の）駅 (tetsudoo no) eki

bus stop バス スタップ
バス停 basutei

taxi stand タクスィ スタンド
タクシー乗り場 takushii noriba

traffic signal トラフィック スィグナゥ
信号 shingoo

railroad crossing レイゥロード クロスィング
踏み切り fumikiri

post office ポウスト アフィス
郵便局 yuubinkyoku

convenience store コンヴィーニエンス ストァ
コンビニ kombini

bank バンク
銀行 ginkoo

police box ポリス バックス
交番 kooban

crosswalk クロスウォーク
横断歩道 oodanhodoo

fire station ファイアァ ステイション
消防署 shooboosho

police station ポリス ステイション
警察署 keisatsusho

intersection インタァセクション
交差点 koosaten

hospital ハスピタゥ
病院 byooin

gas station ギャス ステイション
ガソリンスタンド gasorin stando

pedestrian bridge ペデストリアン ブリッジ
歩道橋 hodookyoo

park パーァク
公園 kooen

public restroom パブリック レストルーム
公衆トイレ kooshuu toire

subway station サブウェイ ステイション
地下鉄駅 chikatetsu eki

underground passage アンダァグラゥンド パスィジ
地下道 chikadoo

★Watch out for bicycles on the sidewalk, where people often ride at high speeds, and accidents involving pedestrians are not uncommon. 歩道をスピードを出して走る自転車が多い。歩行者との接触事故に気を付けよう

turn left イン フロント
ターァン レフト
左に曲がる
hidari ni magaru

in front
イン フロント
前 mae

go straight
ゴウ ストレイト
まっすぐ行く
massugu iku

west ウェスト
西 nishi

north ノーァス
北 kita

left レフト
左 hidari

turn right
ターァン ライト
右に曲がる
migi ni magaru

east イースト
東 higashi

behind ビハインド
後ろ ushiro

go back ゴウ バック
戻る modoru

right ライト
右 migi

south サウス
南 minami

How do I get to the station?
ハウ ドゥ アイ ゲット トゥ ザ ステイション

駅へはどう行けばいいですか？

Eki e wa doo ikeba iidesu ka?

Turn right at the second corner.
ターァン ライト アット ザ セカンド コーァナァ

2つ目の角を右折してすぐですよ

Futatsume no kado o usetsushite sugu desu yo.

Is it far? イズ イット ファーァ↑
そこは遠いんですか？
Soko wa too-indesu ka?

It's very close. イッツ ヴェリィ クロウス
すぐ近くですよ
Sugu chikaku desu yo.

It's a little far. イッツ ア リトゥ ファーァ
ちょっと遠いですね
Chotto too-i desu ne.

I'm lost.
アイム ロスト
道に迷いました
Michi ni mayoimashita.

Where am I?
ウェア アム アイ
ここはどこ？
Koko wa doko?

WORDBANK — Directions 道案内

next to ~	ネクスト トゥ	~の隣に	~ no tonari ni
short cut	ショーァト カット	近道	chikamichi
map	マップ	地図	chizu
here	ヒァァ こっち kocchi	there ゼァァ あっち	acchi
end (of the street)	エンド (オヴ ザ ストリート)	突き当たり	tsukiatari
on the right	オン ザ ライト	右手に	migite ni
on the left	オン ザ レフト	左手に	hidarite ni
diagonally across from ~	ダイアゴヌリィ アクロス フロム	~のはす向かいに	~ no hasumukai ni

★Many buildings and roads do not have street name or address displays. Doing a map search on the web is advised. 道や建物にはあまり道路名や番地表示がない。ネットで地図検索を

Riding buses and taxis

ライディング バスィズ アンド タクスィズ

バス・タクシーに乗ろう
Basu, takushii ni noroo

Where can I catch the bus for ○○?
ウェアァ キャナイ キャッチ ザ バス フォア ○○

○○に行くバスにはどこで乗れますか？

○○ ni iku basu ni wa doko de noremasu ka?

It's past that traffic signal.
イッツ パスト ザット トラフィック スィグナゥ

あの信号の先ですよ。

Ano shingoo no saki desu yo.

Buses with a flat-rate fare generally require you to pay first and board at the front of the bus. If the fare varies by distance, usually you must board in the rear and take a number, and pay the fare displayed on the fare table when you get off. Buses in the Tokyo area also accept IC cards such as PASMO and Suica.

通常、均一運賃のバスは前乗り・先払い。距離によって料金の変わるバスでは、後ろ乗り・あと払いが多い。乗車時に整理券を取り、その番号に従って、降りる際にバス前方の料金表に表示された料金を払う。首都圏ではPASMO、SuicaのようなICカードが使える。

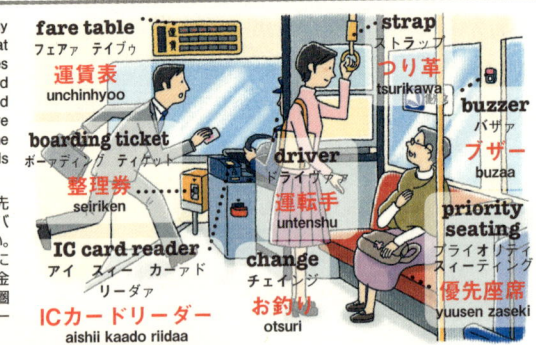

- **fare table** フェアァ テイブゥ — 運賃表 unchinhyoo
- **boarding ticket** ボーディング ティケット — 整理券 seiriken
- **IC card reader** アイ スィー カードゥ リーダァ — ICカードリーダー aishii kaado riidaa
- **strap** ストラップ — つり革 tsurikawa
- **driver** ドライヴァァ — 運転手 untenshu
- **buzzer** バザァ — ブザー buzaa
- **change** チェインジ — お釣り otsuri
- **priority seating** プライオリティ スィーティング — 優先座席 yuusen zaseki

Does this bus stop at ○○?
ダズ ズィス バス スタップ アット ○○↑

このバスは○○に止まりますか？

Kono basu wa ○○ ni tomarimasu ka?

bus route map
バス ラウト マップ

バス路線図

basu rosenzu

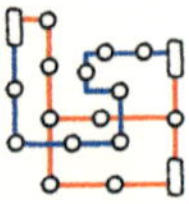

bus stop
バス スタップ

バス停

basutei

get on / get off
ゲット オン／ゲット オフ

乗る／降りる

noru / oriru

WORDBANK — Bus バス

English	Katakana	Japanese	Romaji
timetable	タイムテイブゥ	時刻表	jikokuhyoo
bound for ~	バウンド フォア~	～行きの	~ iki no
via ~	ヴァイア ~	～経由の	~ keiyu no
arrive at ~	アライヴ アット~	～に到着する	~ ni toochaku suru
pass without stopping	パス ウィザウト スタピング	通過する	tsuukasuru
transfer	トランスファァ	乗り換える	norikaeru
miss (a stop)	ミス (ア スタップ)	乗り過ごす	norisugosu
miss (a bus)	ミス (ア バス)	乗り遅れる	noriokureru

★Even in urban areas, buses can be few and far between. Be sure to check bus times for getting home.
都会、地方に関わらず、本数が少ないバス路線も多い。帰りのバスの時間も要チェック

Where should I get off to go to ○○?
ウェアァ シュダイ ゲット オフ トゥ ゴウ トゥ ○○

○○に行くにはどこで降りればいいですか？

○○ ni iku ni wa doko de orireba ii desu ka?

The stop after the next.
ザ スタップ アフタァ ザ ネクスト

次の次の停留所です

Tsugi no tsugi no teiryuujo desu.

Where to, sir / ma'am?
ウェアァ トゥ、サーァ/マーム↑

どちらまででしょうか？

Dochira made deshoo ka?

○○, please.
○○、プリーズ

○○までお願いします

○○ made onegaishimasu.

Could you please hurry?
クジュ プリーズ ハリィ↑

急いでもらえますか？

Isoide moraemasu ka?

Stop at the next signal.
スタップ アット ザ ネクスト スィグナゥ

次の信号で止めてください

Tsugi no shingoo de tomete kudasai.

bus terminal
バス ターァミナゥ

バスターミナル

basu taaminaru

Could you please open the trunk?
クジュ プリーズ オウプン ザ トランク↑

トランクを開けてもらえますか？

Toranku o akete moraemasu ka?

WORDBANK — Taxis タクシー

English	Katakana	Japanese	Romaji
available	アヴェイラブゥ	空車	kuusha
out of service	アウト オヴ サーァヴィス	回送	kaisoo
reserved	リザーァヴド	迎車	geisha
starting fare	スターティング フェアァ	初乗り運賃	hatsunori unchin
extra charge	イクストラ チャーァジ	割増料金	warimashi ryookin
receipt	リスィート	領収書	ryooshuusho
hired car	ハイアァド カーァ	ハイヤー	haiyaa
proxy driver	プロクスィ ドライヴァァ	運転代行	unten daikoo
traffic jam	トラフィック ジャム	渋滞	juutai

COLUMN

Roaming taxis, or "nagashi," are common in cities; but roaming for customers is virtually non-existent in rural areas, where taxis wait at taxi stops or, in some cases, are only available on call. If you call a taxi, an extra charge is incurred. In Japan, taxi doors open automatically.

街で客を拾うために走っているタクシーを「流し」と呼ぶが、地方では流し営業はせず、ほとんどがタクシー乗り場での乗車か呼び出しという地域もある。タクシーを呼ぶ場合は一般に迎車料金がかかる。日本のタクシーは海外ではあまり見られない自動ドアだ。

★If you have been drinking and can no longer drive, make use of a "proxy driver," who will drive your car to your destination. 飲酒などで運転できないときは、代わりに車を目的地まで運んでくれる「運転代行」を利用しよう

Riding trains
ライディング トレインズ
電車に乗ろう
Densha ni noroo

Where is the train for ○○?
ウェアァ イズ ザ トレイン フォア ○○

○○行きの電車にはどこで乗れますか？

○○ iki no densha ni wa doko de noremasu ka?

Platform number 2.
プラットフォーム ナンバァ トゥー

2番線のホームですよ

Nibansen no hoomu desu yo.

Does this train go to ○○?
ダズ ズィス トレイン ゴウ トゥ ○○↑

この電車は○○まで行きますか？

Kono densha wa ○○ made ikimasu ka?

What time does the next express depart?
ワット タイム ダズ ザ ネクスト イクスプレス ディパァト

次の急行は何時に出ますか？

Tsugi no kyuukoo wa nanji ni demasu ka?

🌸 COLUMN

Transfer information
On train station platforms, you will find displays that tell you not only how long it takes to get to your destination but also which cars you should ride to shorten your transfer time. Impatient passengers who don't want to waste a single second of travel time find such displays useful.

乗換案内
都市圏の地下鉄やJRのホームには、駅間の所要時間とともに、各線への乗換に便利な車両がどこかを図示した乗換案内が掲載されている。移動の時間を1秒でも無駄にしたくない人に好評だ。

● **At the train station** 駅構内

- **waiting room** ウェイティング ルーム / 待合室 machiaishitsu
- **transfer point** トランスファー ポイント / 乗換口 norikaeguchi
- **electric bulletin board** イレクトリック ブルティン ボード / 電光掲示板 denkoo keijiban
- **boarding point** ボーディング ポイント / 乗降口 jookooguchi
- **white line** ワイト ライン / 白線 hakusen
- **tracks** トラックス / 線路 senro
- **station employee** ステイション インプロイー / 駅員 ekiin
- **timetable** タイムテイブゥ / 時刻表 jikokuhyoo
- **boarding line indicators** ボーディング ライン インディケイタァズ / 整列乗車のライン seiretsu joosha no rain
- **platform** プラットフォーム / ホーム hoomu
- **ticket-vending machine** ティケットヴェンディング マシーン / 券売機 kembaiki
- **ticket gate** ティケット ゲイト / 改札 kaisatsu
- **kiosk** キーアスク / 売店 baiten

★In Kanto, people stand on the left side of the escalator, and leave the right side open for people in a hurry. In Kansai, people stand on the opposite side. 関東では、エスカレーターでは左に立ち、右を空ける。関西では右側に立つ

IC card アイ スィー カァード **IC カード** aishii kaado	PASMO and Suica are two IC cards that can be used on trains and buses in the greater Tokyo area, and also for shopping. PASMO、Suicaは首都圏の鉄道、バス路線や買物に使えるICカード。	**Japan Rail Pass** ジャパン レイゥ パス **ジャパンレイルパス** japan reiru pasu	Gives foreign travelers unlimited rides on JR trains (incl. most bullet trains), buses, and ferries. 主に外国人旅行者向け。JRのほとんどの新幹線を含む列車やバス、フェリーが乗り放題に。

●Train etiquette 電車でのマナー

*Please refrain from rushing for your car.
プリーズ リフレイン フロム ラシィング フォア ユアァ カーァ
駆け込み乗車はおやめください
Kakekomi joosha wa oyame kudasai.

*Please line up to get on the train.
プリーズ ライン アップ トゥ ゲット オン ザ トレイン
整列乗車にご協力ください
Seiretsu joosha ni gokyooryoku kudasai.

*Please refrain from speaking on your cell phone on the train.
プリーズ リフレイン フロム スピーキング オン ユアァ セゥ フォウン オン ザ トレイン
社内では携帯電話での通話はご遠慮ください
Shanai de wa keitaidenwa de no tsuuwa wa goenryo kudasai.

*Please make space for others to sit.
プリーズ メイク スペイス フォア アザァズ トゥ スィット
座席は譲り合っておかけください
Zaseki wa yuzuriatte okake kudasai.

How long does it take to ○○? ハウ ロング ダズ イット テイク トゥ ○○ **○○までどのくらいかかりますか？** ○○ made donokurai kakarimasuka?	**I lost my ticket.** アイ ロスト マイ ティケット **切符をなくしてしまいました** Kippu o nakushite shimaimashita.

COLUMN

Railway companies offer discount book tickets and daily passes, and there are also passes that allow you to ride train lines of different companies. The "Seishun 18 Ticket," a one-day pass that allows you to ride any JR local express train during limited times of the year, is popular among backpackers.

鉄道各社では回数券、乗り放題の1日乗車券などを用意している。異なる鉄道会社の路線も自由に乗り降りできるパスもある。また、全国のJRの普通快速列車が特定期間乗り放題の「青春18きっぷ」は、バックパッカーにも人気。

WORDBANK Train 電車

local	ロウカゥ	各駅	kakueki
limited express	リミティド イクスプレス	特急	tokkyuu
refund	リファンド	払い戻し	haraimodoshi
one-way	ワンウェイ	片道の	katamichi no
round trip	ラウンド トリップ	往復の	oofuku no
bullet train	ブレット トレイン	新幹線	shinkansen
missing your stop	ミスィング ユアァ スタップ	乗り越し	norikoshi
stopover	スタプオウヴァァ	途中下車	tochuugesha

★Large metropolitan areas have a complex network of JR, private railway, and subway trains, so it's a good idea to do a web train line search. 大都市には、JRや私鉄、地下鉄が複雑に乗り入れている。ネットで路線検索を

Riding cars and bicycles
ライディング カーアズ アンド バイスィクゥズ

自動車・自転車に乗ろう
Jidoosha, jitensha ni noroo

I'd like to rent a car.
アイド ライク トゥ レント ア カーア

レンタカーの予約をしたいのですが
Rentakaa no yoyaku o shitai no desu ga.

What kind of car would you like?
ワット カインド オヴ カーア ウジュ ライク

どんな車種をご希望ですか？
Donna shashu o gokiboo desu ka?

car navigation system
カーア ナヴィゲイション スィステム
カーナビ
kaanabi

rear-view mirror
リアヴュー ミラァ
バックミラー
bakku miraa

side mirror
サイド ミラァ
サイドミラー
saido miraa

speedometer
スピーダミタァ
速度計
sokudokei

horn
ホーアン
クラクション
kurakushon

turn signal
ターアン スィグナゥ
ウィンカー
uinkaa

seatbelt
スィートベゥト
シートベルト
shiito beruto

steering wheel
スティーリング ウィーゥ
ハンドル
handoru

passenger seat
パスィンジャァ スィート
助手席
joshuseki

brake
ブレイク
ブレーキ
bureeki

gas pedal
ギャス ペダゥ
アクセル
akuseru

automatic
オートマティック
オートマチック車
ootomachikku sha

manual
マニュアゥ
マニュアル車
manyuaru sha

4-wheel drive
フォーアウイーゥ ドライヴ
4WD
yondaburudii

🌸 COLUMN

Crosswalk music
For the visually-impaired, Japanese traffic signals would commonly play songs such as "Tōryanse" or "Kokyō no sora" when the light turned green; but in recent years, these songs have been replaced by bird chirping sounds or mechanical-sounding signals.

横断歩道の音楽
視覚障害者のために、青信号のときには「とおりゃんせ」や「故郷の空」を流していることが多かったが、最近では鳥のさえずりや機械的な信号音にとって代わられている。

WORDBANK — Car life カーライフ

English	Katakana	Japanese	Romaji
parking lot	パーキング ラット	駐車場	chuushajoo
expressway	イクスプレスウェイ	高速道路	koosoku dooro
speed limit	スピード リミット	制限速度	seigen sokudo
drop-off charge	ドラブオフ チャーァジ	乗り捨て料金	norishite ryookin
run out of gas	ラン アウト オヴ ギャス	ガス欠になる	gasuketsu ni naru
get a flat tire	ゲット ア フラット タイアァ	パンクする	panku suru
have a dead battery	ハヴ ア デッド バテリィ	バッテリーが上がる	batterii ga agaru
radiator	ラディエイタァ	ラジエーター	rajieetaa

★ "Handoru," "bakku miraa," "kurakushon," "gasonrin sutando" are Japlish words.
ハンドル、バックミラー、クラクション、ガソリンスタンドなどは和製英語だ

gas station
ギャス　ステイション
ガソリンスタンド
gasorin sutando

Fill it up with regular.
フィゥ　イット　アップ　ウィズ　レギュラァ
レギュラー満タンで
Regyuraa mantan de.

Cash or charge?
キャッシュ　オアァ　チャーァジ
お支払いはカードですか、現金ですか？
Oshiharai wa kaado desu ka, genkin desu ka?

---

premium
プリミアム
ハイオク
haioku

recharge
リチャーァジ
充電する
juuden suru

Please wash my car.
プリーズ　ワッシュ　マイ　カーァ
洗車をお願いします
Sensha o onegaishimasu.

In Japan, cars drive on the left side of the road.
イン　ジャパン　カーァズ　ドライヴ　オン　ザ　レフト　サイド　オヴ　ザ　ロウド
日本では自動車は左側通行です
Nihon de wa jidoosha wa hidarigawa tsuukoo desu.

pedestrian
ペデストリアン
歩行者
hokoosha

Is there a parking lot around here?
イズ　ゼアァ　ア　パーァキング　ラット　アラウンド　ヒアァ↑
このあたりに駐車場はありますか？
Konoatari ni chuushajoo wa arimasu ka?

sidewalk
サイドウォーク
歩道
hodoo

---

shopping bike
シャピング　バイク
ママチャリ
mamachari

Bicycles, mainly for women, with large baskets in front. Weighing around 20kg, they offer a stable ride even at low speeds. Some are also equipped with child seats.

主に女性向けのカゴ付き自転車。重量が20kg程度でゆっくり走っても安定感がある。幼児用座席の付いたものも。

🌸 COLUMN

Bicycles in Japan
In urban areas, many people ride their bikes to and from the train station as part of their daily commute, resulting in a shortage of bicycle parking around stations. Bicycles in "No bicycle parking" zones are regularly removed, and bicycle owners must pay to claim their removed bicycles.

日本の自転車事情
都市部では、通勤通学に駅まで自転車を利用する人が多く、駅周辺の駐輪場不足が問題に。駐輪禁止区間の自転車は定期的に取り締まられ、撤去される。撤去自転車引取りには手数料がかかる。

Rules for riding bicycles
In Japan, many people ride their bikes on the sidewalk, but cyclists aged 13 and over are actually supposed to ride on the left side of car lanes. Giving someone a ride and riding while carrying an umbrella or using a cell phone are also prohibited by law, and subject to fine.

自転車の走行ルール
日本では歩道を走行する自転車が多いが、本来は13歳以上は車道の左側を走らなければならない。また、2人乗り、傘や携帯電話を使用しながらの運転も法律上禁止され、違反すると罰金。

★Many gas stations in Japan will clean your ashtray and wipe your windows free of charge while filling your car with gas. 日本のガソリンスタンドでは、給油中に灰皿の掃除、窓拭きなどの無料サービスをしてくれる

Signs around town
サインズ アラウンド タウン
街で見かける標識
Machi de mikakeru hyooshiki

What does this sign mean?
ワット ダズ ズィス サイン ミーン
この標識はどういう意味ですか？
Kono hyooshiki wa dooiu imi desu ka?

It means ○○.
イット ミーンズ ○○
○○を表しています
○○ o arawashite imasu.

●**Traffic signs**　交通標識

Bicycles and Pedestrians Only
バイスィクルズ アンド ペデストリアンズ オンリー
自転車・歩行者専用
jitensha hokoosha sen-yoo

Stop
スタップ
止まれ
tomare

Yield
イールド
徐行
jokoo

No Vehicle Entry
ノウ ヴィーイクル エンタリィ
車両進入禁止
sharyoo shin-nyuu kinshi

Closed to Vehicle Traffic
クロウズド トゥ ヴィーイクル トラフィック
車両通行止め
sharyoo tsuukoodome

No Stopping / Parking
ノウ スタピング／パーキング
駐停車禁止
chuuteisha kinshi

One way
ワン ウェイ
一方通行
ippoo tsuukoo

Road Under Construction
ロウド アンダア コンストラクション
道路工事中
doorokoojichuu

No Crossing
ノウ クロスィング
横断禁止
oodan kinshi

Road Narrows Ahead ロウド ナロウズ アヘッド 幅員減少 hukuin genshoo 	**School / Kindergarten Zone** スクウ／キンダァガァテン ゾウン 学校・幼稚園等あり gakkoo, yoochien too ari 
Caution: Side Wind コーション：サイド ウィンド 横風注意 yokokaze chuui 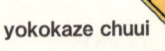	**Slippery** スリパリィ すべりやすい suberiyasui 

🌸 COLUMN
What is "taspo"?
Taspo is an IC card photo ID required for buying cigarettes at vending machines. It can also be used as e-money at vending machines. To apply, fill out an application (available at a cigarette shops or online), and mail it along with your photo and ID.

taspoとは
自動販売機でタバコを買う際に必要な、顔写真付きの成人識別Cカード。自動販売機で使える電子マネーの機能もある。申込書はタバコ店やインターネットで入手し、身分証明書・顔写真を添えて郵送する。

24　★The "go" light on traffic signals in Japan is green, but is referred to as an "*ao shingō*," or "blue light."
日本の信号機では「進め」の色は緑だが、「青信号」などのように、緑ではなく「青」と呼ばれる

What does that say?
ワット ダズ ザット セイ

あれは何て書いてあるんですか？
Are wa nante kaite arundesu ka?

It says "Danger: Flammable."
イット セッズ "デインジャ：フレイマブゥ"

「火気厳禁」と書いてあるんですよ
Kakigenkin to kaite arundesu yo.

Emergency Exit イマーァジュンスィ イクズィット 非常口 hijooguchi 	**No Shoes** ノウ シューズ 土足厳禁  dosoku genkin 	**No Smoking** ノウ スモウキング 禁煙 kin-en 
No Trespassing ノウ トレスパスィング 立ち入り禁止  tachiiri kinshi	**Danger: High Voltage** デインジャァ：ハイ ヴォゥティッジ 危険　高電圧 kiken kooden-atsu	**Priority Seat** プライオリティ スィート 優先席 yuusenseki
Cell Phone Use Prohibited セゥ フォウン ユーズ プロウヒビティッド 携帯電話使用禁止 keitaidenwa shiyoo kinshi	**Open** オウプン 開く  hiraku	**Close** クロウズ 閉まる shimaru

No Urinating
ノウ ユレネイティング

立ち小便禁止

tachishooben kinshi

The "*torii*" (shrine archway) symbol found on walls and electric poles means "no urinating." The implication is that you should not urinate on *torii* because it represents a sacred place.

民家の塀や電柱などに書かれた鳥居のマークは、「立ち小便禁止」を意味する。「神様のいる場所である鳥居におしっこをかけてはいけません」ということを暗に示したサイン。

Push プッシュ 押す  osu	**Pull** プゥ 引く  hiku
Vacant ヴェイカント 空車 kuusha	**Full** フゥ 満車  mansha

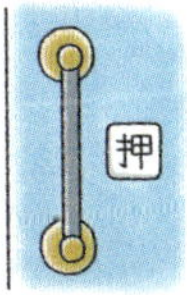

★"開" and "閉" can be seen on buttons for opening and closing elevator doors. People often push "close" before the door closes automatically. 「開」「閉」はドアの表示に見られる。自動で閉まる前に「閉」を押す人が多い

Staying at hotels and other facilities

ステイング アット ホテゥズ
アンド ファスィリティズ

宿泊施設に泊まろう
Shukuhaku shisetsu ni tomaroo

I'd like to make a reservation.
アイド ライク トゥ メイク ア リザァヴェイション

予約をお願いしたいのですが

Yoyaku o onegaishitai no desu ga.

Do you have any double rooms available on ~ ?
ドゥ ユ ハヴ エニィ ダブゥ ルームズ アヴェイラブゥ オン ~↑

～日にダブルルームは空いていますか？

~ nichi ni daburu ruumu wa aite imasu ka?

Yes, we do.
イェス ウィ ドゥ

はい、ございます

Hai, gozaimasu.

I'm sorry, there are no vacancies.
アイム サリィ ゼアァ アァ ノウ ヴェイカンスィーズ

申し訳ありませんが満室となっております

Mooshiwake arimasen ga manshitsu to natte orimasu.

---

business hotel
ビズィネス ホテゥ

ビジネスホテル

bijinesu hoteru

Located near train stations, they are small (usually one room) and relatively cheap, and used mainly by people travelling on business.

駅前などの交通の便のいい場所にあるシングルルーム中心のホテルで、比較的安い。主にビジネスマンの出張で利用される。

bed and breakfast
ベッド アンド ブレクファスト

民宿

minshuku

These small-scale Japanese-style accommodations are mainly used for recreational purposes. Part of their appeal is the family-like service and low price.

小規模の和風の宿泊施設で、レジャー目的の利用が主体。家庭的なサービスと低料金が魅力。

no-frills lodging house
ノウフリゥズ ラジング ハウス

簡易宿泊所

kan-i shukuhakujo

Places that previously served mainly as lodgings for day laborers, many have renovated and become popular among backpackers as cheap, safe places to stay.

元々は日雇い労働者向けだったが、近年改装するところが増え、安く安全な宿としてバックパッカーに人気に。

capsule hotel
キャプスゥ ホテゥ

カプセルホテル

kapuseru hoteru

Usually comprised of a large room lined with two levels of curtained beds, each equipped with a small TV. Some also have a communal bath.

通常上下2段のカプセル状のベッドにカーテンがかかったものが大部屋に並ぶ。中には小型テレビもあり、共同浴場が併設されている。

WORDBANK — Accommodation 宿泊

single room	スィングゥ ルーム	シングルルーム	shinguru ruumu
twin room	トゥイン ルーム	ツインルーム	tsuin ruumu
registration card	レジストレイション カァード	宿泊カード	shukuhaku kaado
non-smoking room	ノンスモウキング ルーム	禁煙ルーム	kin-en ruumu
valuables	ヴァリュアブゥズ	貴重品	kichoohin
with breakfast	ウィズ ブレクファスト	朝食付き	chooshoku tsuki
itemized receipt	アイテマイズド リスィート	明細書	meisaisho
shuttle bus	シャトゥ バス	送迎バス	soogee basu

★ "Guest houses" are no-frills lodging houses for foreigners, but they are also used by Japanese people traveling cheaply. 「ゲストハウス」と称する外国人向けの簡易宿泊所は、格安旅行をする日本人も利用

lobby
ラビィ
ロビー
robii

I have a reservation.
アイ ハヴ ア リザァヴェイション
今晩部屋を予約してあるのですが
Komban heya o yoyakushitearu no desu ga.

What's the name?
ワッツ ザ ネイム
ご予約のお名前は？
Goyoyaku no onamae wa?

front desk
フラント デスク
フロント
furonto

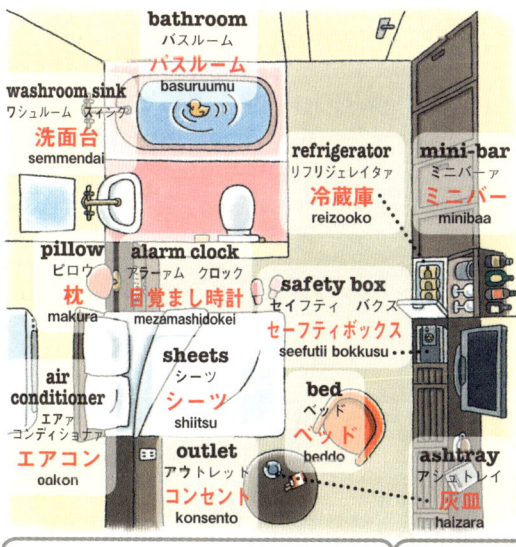

bathroom バスルーム / basuruumu
washroom sink ワシュルーム スィンク / 洗面台 / semmendai
refrigerator リフリジェレイタァ / 冷蔵庫 / reizooko
mini-bar ミニバァー / ミニバー / minibaa
pillow ピロウ / 枕 / makura
alarm clock アラーァム クロック / 目覚まし時計 / mezamashidokei
safety box セイフティ バクス / セーフティボックス / seefutii bokkusu
air conditioner エアァ コンディショナァ / エアコン / eakon
sheets シーツ / shiitsu
bed ベッド / beddo
outlet アウトレット / コンセント / konsento
ashtray アシュトレイ / 灰皿 / haizara

room with a view
ルーム ウィズ ア ヴュー
眺めのいい部屋
nagame no ii heya

wake-up call
ウェイクアップ コーゥ
モーニングコール
mooningu kooru

There's no hot water.
ゼアァズ ノウ ハット ウォータァ
お湯が出ません
Oyu ga demasen.

The toilet doesn't flush.
ザ トイレット ダズント フラッシュ
トイレが流れないのですが
Toire ga nagarenai no desu ga.

I locked myself out of my room.
アイ ロックト マイセゥフ アウト オヴ マイ ルーム
部屋に鍵を置き忘れてしまいました
Heya ni kagi o okiwasurete shimaimashita.

The light bulb has burnt out.
ザ ライト バゥブ ハズ バーァント アウト
電球が切れたのですが
Denkyuu ga kireta no desu ga.

The people in the next room are noisy.
ザ ピープゥ イン ザ ネクスト ルーム ァァ ノイズィィ
隣の部屋がうるさいのですが
Tonari no heya ga urusai no desu ga.

★ "*Minshuku*" in Western-style buildings serving Western-style food are referred to as "pensions."
民宿の中でも、特に西洋風の建物で西洋風の食事を提供する宿泊施設を「ペンション」と呼ぶ

Etiquette at Japanese-style inns

エティケット アット
ジャパニーズ スタイゥ インズ

旅館のマナー・過ごし方
Ryokan no manaa, sugoshikata

Please take off your footwear here.
プリーズ テイク オフ ユアァ フトウェアァ ヒアァ

こちらで履物をお脱ぎください
Kochira de hakimono o onugi kudasai.

Please enter your name and address.
プリーズ エンタァ ユアァ ネイム アンド アドレス

宿帳にご記入をお願いします
Yadochoo ni gokinyuu o onegaishimasu.

🌸 COLUMN

Tipping at Japanese-style inns
When showing you to your room, the *nakai* may give an explanation of the facilities and offer tea and sweets. Whether or not you offer a tip when she leaves the room is a matter of personal choice; but if you ask for a special favor or your child causes some damage, you should leave a tip of 1,000 or 3,000 yen. Wrapping it in "*kaishi*" paper or (if *kaishi* is not available) tissue is advised.

旅館での心づけ
部屋に通されると、仲居さんが旅館内施設を説明してくれたり、お茶と和菓子を出してくれたりする。仲居さんが部屋を出る際には「心づけ（チップ）」を渡すかどうかは個人の気持ち次第。仲居さんや女将に無理を言って部屋を変えてもらうとか、子供が障子を破ったとかいった場合は渡すようにしよう。金額は1,000円か3,000円程度。お金は懐紙で包むのが理想だが、なければティッシュでもいい。

- **proprietress** プロプライエトレス 女将 okami
- **manager** マニジャァ 番頭 bantoo
- **waitress** ウェイトレス 仲居 nakai
- **reception desk** リセプション デスク 帳場 chooba
- **hotel register** ホテゥ レジスタァ 宿帳 yadochoo
- **shoe caretaker** シュー ケアァテイカァ 下足番 gesokuban
- **clogs** クロッグズ 下駄 geta

Some *ryokan* require guests to take off their shoes at the entrance. If someone is there to take care of your shoes, you do not have to arrange them yourself; but be sure to say, "*Onegaishimasu* (Please)." Let the inn staff carry your luggage for you. Be aware that entering a false name and address in the register is against the law.

旅館では玄関で靴を脱ぐ場合がある。出迎えてくれる仲居さんや下足番がいる場合は、靴は脱いだまま揃えずに上がっていい。ただし、「お願いします」とひとこと声をかけよう。また、重い荷物は運んでもらう。宿帳に虚偽の住所氏名を書くのは法律違反となるので注意しよう。

● Japanese room etiquette 和室のマナー

Do not put your baggage in the alcove.
ドゥ ナット プット ユアァ バギッジ イン ズィ アゥコウヴ
床の間に荷物を置かない
Tokonoma ni nimotsu o okanai.

Put wet towels on hangers.
プット ウェット タウェゥズ オン ハンガァズ
濡れたタオルはタオルかけに
Nureta taoru wa taorukake ni.

Do not step on thresholds or tatami edges.
ドゥ ナット ステップ オン スレシホウゥズ オアァ タタミ エッジズ
畳のへりや敷居を踏まない
Tatami no heri ya shikii o fumanai.

Do not step on floor cushions.
ドゥ ナット ステップ オン フローァ クシォンズ
座布団を踏まない
Zabuton o fumanai.

★ Many Japanese-style inns do not have automatic locks on the doors. Keep your valuables at the reception desk or in a safety box. 旅館の部屋はオートロックでない場合も。貴重品は帳場かセーフティボックスへ

How do you wear yukata?
ハウ ドゥ ユ ウェアァ ユカタ

浴衣はどうやって着るのですか？

Yukata wa dooyatte kiru no desu ka?

COLUMN

Billing at Japanese-style inns
People staying at Japanese-style inns are generally charged for "one night and two meals"; however, in an effort to make rates more transparent and cater to guests who do not need meals, there are also places that have separate rates for boarding and meals.

旅館の宿泊料金
夕食と朝食付きの「一泊二食」の宿泊料金が一般的。しかし料金設定を明瞭にし、夕食は不要などの要望に応えるため、宿泊と食事を別々に設定した「泊食分離」を進めている旅館もある。

How to wear *yukata*
ハウ トゥ ウェアァ ユカタ

浴衣の着方

yukata no kikata

At *ryokan*, *yukata* can be worn casually, with the sash tied in front. However, you should put the left side in front; and women should let it hang slightly at the back of the neck, while men should wear the sash low, at the waist. If you are not sure how to wear *yukata*, feel free to consult with the *nakai*.

旅館で用意されている浴衣は、帯を前に結ぶ気軽な着方でいい。ただし、左前にする、女性は襟足を少し抜く、男性は帯を腰の位置で（下げ気味に）巻く、というルールだけは守るようにしたい。わからなければ仲居さんに遠慮なく相談してみよう。

Feel free to take a bath before dinner.
フィーゥ フリー トゥ テイク ア バス ビフォアァ ディナァ

夕食の前にお風呂へどうぞ

Yuushoku no mae ni ofuro e doozo.

Bath times are different for men and women, so check with the *nakai* to ensure that it doesn't overlap with your dinner time.

大浴場は、通常男女別に使える時間が決まっているので、夕食の時間と重ならないよう仲居さんに確認しておこう。

Dinner will be served in your room.
ディナァ ウィゥ ビ サーァヴド イン ユアァ ルーム

夕食はお部屋で召し上がっていただきます

Yuushoku wa oheya de meshiagatte itadakimasu.

Having your meal brought to your room is called "*heyashoku*." *Heyashoku* allows you to enjoy meals at your leisure without worrying about other guests.

部屋に食事を運んできてもらうのを「部屋食」という。回りを気にせず、のんびり食事を楽しめるのが魅力。

Your food is here.
ユアァ フード イズ ヒアァ

お食事をお持ちしました

Oshokuji o omochi shimashita.

May I lay out the futons?
メイ アイ レイ アウト ザ フトンズ↑

お布団を敷いてよろしいですか？

Ofuton o shiite yoroshii desu ka?

COLUMN

Japanese food etiquette
* Don't mix wasabi and soy sauce together. Place wasabi on sashimi and dip the sashimi in soy sauce.
* When you finish eating the top half of grilled fish, remove the bone and eat the rest without turning it over.
* Put lids back on bowls when you are finished.

覚えておきたい和食のマナー
* わさびはしょうゆに溶かさず、刺身などに載せてから、しょうゆをつける
* 焼き魚は上半分を食べたあとはひっくり返さずに骨を外して食べる
* お椀の蓋は食後には元に戻す

★You can have the "*nakai*" lay out your futons for you. In the morning, just straighten them up a bit and fold them in half. 布団は仲居さんに敷いてもらえる。朝は軽く整えて、二つ折りにしておくだけでいい

Visiting a hot spring spa
ヴィズィティング ア ハット スプリング スパ

温泉に行こう
Onsen ni ikoo

Have you ever been to a Japanese hot spring spa?
ハヴ ユ エヴァァ ビン トゥ ア ジャパニーズ ハット スプリング スパ↑

日本の温泉に行ったことはありますか？
Nihon no onsen ni itta koto wa arimasu ka?

What hot spring area do you recommend?
ワット ハット スプリング エリァア ドゥ ユ レコメンド

おすすめの温泉地はどこですか？
Osusume no onsenchi wa doko desu ka?

What kind of effect does that hot spring have?
ワット カインド オヴ エフェクト ダズ ザット ハット スプリング ハヴ

その温泉にはどんな効能があるんですか？
Sono onsen ni wa donna koonoo ga arundesu ka?

sore muscles
ソアァ マスゥズ

筋肉痛
kinnikutsuu

It is good for neuralgia.
イット イズ グッド フォア ニューラゥジャ

神経痛に効くんですよ
Shinkeitsuu ni kikundesu yo.

cold hands and feet
コウゥド ハンズ アンド フィート

冷え性
hieshoo

hot spring water deposits
ハット スプリング ウォータァ ディパズィット

湯の花
yunohana

effective for beautifying skin
エフェクティヴ フォア ビューティファイング スキン

美肌効果がある
bihadakooka ga aru

I feel light-headed.
アイ フィーゥ ライトヘディド

のぼせてしまいました
Nobosete shimaimashita.

mixed bathing
ミクスト ベイズィング

混浴
kon-yoku

You shouldn't stay in the bath too long.
ユ シュドゥント ステイ イン ザ バス トゥー ロング

長時間湯船に浸からないほうがいいですよ
Choojikan yubune ni tsukaranai hoo ga ii desu yo.

★Many Japanese-style inns have "private baths (family baths)" that you can use with your partner or family.
家族やカップルだけで利用できる「貸切風呂（家族風呂）」を設置している旅館も多い

This spa uses free-flowing hot spring water.
ズィス スパ ユーズィズ フリーフロウイング ハット スプリング ウォータァ

この温泉は源泉かけ流しです
Kono onsen wa gensen kakenagashi desu.

private bath
プライヴェット バス

貸切風呂

kashikiri buro

go to a day spa
ゴウ トゥア デイ スパ

日帰り温泉に行く

higaeri onsen ni iku

🌸 COLUMN

Free-flowing hot spring water
This means that water is taken directly from hot springs into the bath without adding any other water, and is allowed to flow out, rather than circulated in the bath. Many bathing facilities in places with a limited hot spring water supply take the water overflow and return it to the bath after filtrating it and adding disinfectants; but recently there has been renewed interest in fresh "free-flowing hot spring water."

源泉かけ流し
源泉から湧き出た温泉に加水せずに浴槽に汲み入れ、その湯を循環させずに流したままにすること。湧出量の限られた温泉では浴槽からあふれた湯をろ過して消毒薬などを混ぜて浴槽に戻す「循環風呂」にしている入浴施設も多いなか、新鮮な「かけ流し」に注目が集まっている。

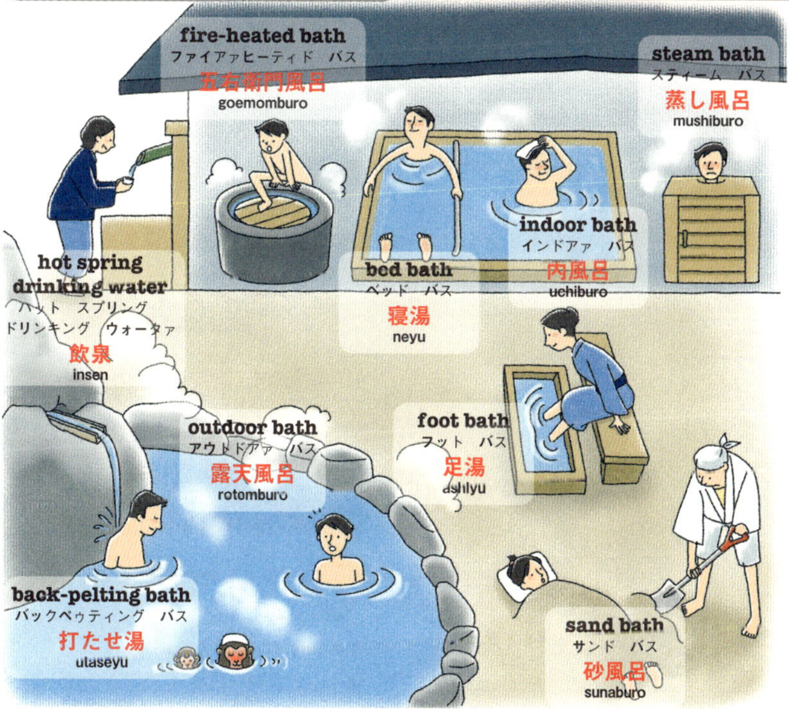

---

fire-heated bath
ファイァヒーティド バス
五右衛門風呂
goemomburo

steam bath
スティーム バス
蒸し風呂
mushiburo

indoor bath
インドァ バス
内風呂
uchiburo

bed bath
ベッド バス
寝湯
neyu

hot spring drinking water
ハット スプリング ドリンキング ウォータァ
飲泉
insen

outdoor bath
アウトドァ バス
露天風呂
rotomburo

foot bath
フット バス
足湯
ashiyu

back-pelting bath
バックペッティング バス
打たせ湯
utaseyu

sand bath
サンド バス
砂風呂
sunaburo

★ "Day-trip hot spring" spas, which are used only for bathing and have no sleeping accommodations, are convenient and popular. 宿泊施設のない、温泉入浴だけの「日帰り温泉」施設も手軽で人気になっている

Hot spring bath etiquette

ハット スプリング
バス エティケット
温泉のマナー
Onsen no manaa

Please wash your body before entering the bath.
プリーズ ワッシュ ユアァ バディ ビフォァ エンタリング ザ バス

最初に体を洗ってください
Saisho ni karada o aratte kudasai.

May I add water?
メイ アイ アッド ウォータァ↑

お水を足していいですか？
Omizu o tashite ii desu ka?

No way! You can't change the temperature of the water.
ノウ ウェイ ユ キャント チェインジ ザ テンパラチャァ オヴ ザ ウォータァ

とんでもない！　お湯の温度は変えちゃいけないんですよ
Tondemo nai! Oyu no ondo wa kaecha ikenaindesu yo.

●**Rules for healthy bathing**　健康的な入浴のルール

* **Avoid bathing when hungry and immediately after eating / drinking.**
アヴォイド ベイズィング ウェン ハングリィ アンド イミディエトリィ アフタァ イーティング/ドリンキング
空腹時、食事・飲食直後の入浴は避ける
Kuufukuji, shokuji, inshokuchokugo no nyuuyoku wa sakeru.

* **After bathing in hot water for 3 minutes, rest for 5 minutes. Do this up to 3 times.**
アフタァ ベイズィング イン ハット ウォータァ フォァ スリー ミニッツ レスト フォァ ファイヴ ミニッツ ドゥ ズィス アップ トゥ スリー タイムズ
熱い湯には3分浸かって5分休憩を3セットまで
Atsui yu ni wa sampun tsukatte gofun kyuukei o sansetto made.

* **Take no more than 3 baths a day.**
テイク ノウ モアァ ザン スリー バス ア デイ
入浴は1日3回まで
Nyuuyoku wa ichinichi sankai made.

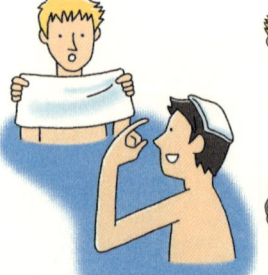

Where do I put the towel?
ウェアァ ドゥ アイ プット ザ タウェゥ

タオルはどこに置いといたらいいかな？
Taoru wa doko ni oitoitara ii kana?

You can place it on your head.
ユ キャン プレイス イット オン ユアァ ヘッド

頭に載せるといいよ
Atama ni noseru to ii yo.

★Placing a cold towel on your head is one way to keep yourself from feeling light-headed.
冷たい水で絞ったタオルを頭に載せておくのは、のぼせ予防にもなる

① Remove slippers when entering the changing room.

② Since changing rooms often have no lockers, leave valuables in your room's safety box.

③ Take one small towel with you to the bath area. Swimsuits are usually prohibited. If someone is already in the bath, nod in greeting.

④ Using a bath basin, splash hot water from the bath onto your body, starting away from the heart. This is done not only for cleaning purposes but also to adjust your body to the hot water.

⑤ Wash your body and hair. Most baths are equipped with shampoo, rinse and body soap. Be careful to avoid splashing water on other people. After washing, rinse off the bath basin and stool.

⑥ When sitting in the bath, be careful not to let your towel or hair touch the bathwater. Don't add cold water to the bath, even if it is hot.

⑦ If you are concerned about hygiene or the water's chemical content, rinse off with clean hot water after bathing.

⑧ Wipe your body with your small towel before leaving the bath area.

① 脱衣所に入るときスリッパを脱ぐ

② ロッカーがないことも。貴重品は持ってこない

③ 浴室に入るときには小さいタオルを1枚持参。もちろん水着は禁止されているところが多い。先に入っている人がいたら会釈しよう

④ 「かけ湯」をする。湯船から風呂桶にお湯を汲んで、心臓に遠いところからかけていく。体をきれいにするだけでなく、お湯に体を慣らす意味がある

⑤ 体や髪を洗う。通常シャンプー・コンディショナー・ボディーソープは備え付けてある。ほかの人に水しぶきや泡がかからないように注意。風呂いすや風呂桶は使い終わったあと水で流しておく

⑥ 湯船に浸かるとき、タオルや髪がお湯に浸からないように注意。熱くても冷水を足さない

⑦ 衛生面が気になるとき、また泉質が強いときには最後に「上がり湯」（清水）をかける

⑧ 浴室から出るときには持参したタオルで体を拭いてから

Do not put the towel in the bathwater!

ドゥ ナット プット ザ タウェゥ イン ザ バスウォータァ

タオルをお湯に浸けないで！

Taoru o oyu ni tsukenai de!

Thoroughly rinse off soap.

サーロウリィ リンス オフ ソウプ

せっけんをよく流してください

Sekken o yoku nagashite kudasai.

★ Sometimes, even if the changing rooms are separate for men and women, outdoor baths are mixed.
露天風呂は、脱衣所が男女別でも浴室は男女一緒（混浴）になっていることがある

Enjoying recreational activities

インジョイング リクリエイショナゥ アクティヴィティィ

余暇・娯楽を楽しもう

Yoka, goraku o tanoshimoo

Do you want to go see a movie tonight?
ドゥ ユ ワント トゥ ゴウ スィー ア ムーヴィ トゥナイト↑

今夜映画を観に行かない?

Kon-ya eiga o mini ikanai?

Sounds good. What should we see?
サウンズ グッド ワット シュド ウィ スィー

いいわね。何を観ようか?

Ii wane. Nani o miyoo ka?

---

movie theater
ムーヴィ スィアタァ

映画館
eigakan

ticket box
ティケット バクス

チケット売り場
chiketto uriba

buy tickets online
バイ ティケッツ オンライン

インターネットでチケットを買う
intaanetto de chiketto o kau

WORDBANK — Movies 映画

English	カタカナ	日本語	Romaji
advance ticket	アドヴァンス ティケット	前売券	maeuri ken
same-day ticket	セイムデイ ティケット	当日券	toojitsu ken
playing time	プレイング タイム	上演時間	jooei jikan
subtitles	サブタイトゥズ	字幕	jimaku
dubbed	ダブド	吹き替え	fukikae
rent	レント	借りる	kariru
return	リターァン	返却する	henkyaku suru
late fee	レイト フィー	延滞料金	entai ryookin
new release	ニュー リリース	新作	shinsaku

COLUMN

"With subtitles" or "dubbed"? For people who can't read Chinese characters or keep up with subtitles, dubbed movies are becoming more popular in Japan. "Super-translations" that put understanding before accuracy are also gaining attention.

字幕か吹き替えか?
日本では、字幕の漢字が読めない、字幕のスピードについていけないなどの理由から、字幕より吹き替えを好む人が増えてきた。また正確さよりもニュアンスや分かりやすさを優先させた「超訳」も話題になっている。

Your membership card, please.
ユア メンバシップ カァード プリーズ

会員証をお願いします

kaiinshoo o onegaishimasu.

DVD rental shop
ディーヴィーディー レンタゥ シャップ

DVDレンタルショップ
diibuidii rentaru shoppu

Will this be for one week?
ウィゥ ズィス ビ フォァ ワン ウィーク↑

貸し出しは1週間でよろしいですか?

Kashidashi wa isshuukan de yoroshii desu ka?

delivery rental
ディリヴァリィ レンタゥ

宅配レンタル
takuhai rentaru

★At movie theatres nationwide, tickets are sold at the discount price of 1,000 yen on the 1st of every month ("Service Day"). 毎月1日を「サービスデー」とし、映画鑑賞を1000円とする割引がほぼ全国で行われている

Let's go to the amusement park this Sunday.
レッツ ゴウ トゥ ズィ アミューズメント パーァク ズィス サンデイ

今度の日曜日は遊園地に行こうよ
Kondo no nichiyoobi wa yuuenchi ni ikoo yo.

Let's ride the ○○ next!
レッツ ライド ザ ○○ ネクスト

次は○○に乗ろう！
Tsugi wa ○○ ni noroo!

entrance fee
エントランス フィー

入場料
nyuujooryoo

● **Amusement park rides** 遊園地の乗り物

haunted house
ホーンティド ハウス
お化け屋敷
obake yashiki

roller coaster
ロウラァ コウスタァ
ジェットコースター
jetto koosutaa

Ferris wheel
フェリス ウィーゥ
観覧車
kanransha

arcade
アーァケイド
ゲームセンター
geemu sentaa

tea cup
ティー カップ
ティーカップ
tii kappu

merry-go-round
メリィゴウラウンド
メリーゴーランド
meriigoorando

go cart
ゴウ カート
ゴーカート
goo kaato

What do you do on weekends?
ワット ドゥ ユ ドゥ オン ウィークエンズ

週末は何をしていますか？
Shuumatsu wa nani o shite imasu ka?

meet friends
ミート フレンズ
友達に会う
tomodachi ni au

I go to the gym.
アイ ゴウ トゥ ザ ジム

ジムに行っています
Jimu ni kayotte imasu.

surf the net
サーァフ ザ ネット
ネットサーフィンする
netto saafin suru

manga café
マンガ キャフェイ
マンガ喫茶
manga kissa

go to the library
ゴウ トゥ ザ ライブラリィ
図書館に行く
toshokan ni iku

go shopping
ゴウ シャピング
買物に行く
kaimono ni iku

★Many "manga cafés" not only have comic books and magazines but also offer services such as internet surfing and DVD watching. 多くの「マンガ喫茶」では、漫画や雑誌だけでなくインターネットやDVDなども見られる

Getting Things
買おう

Free tissue 無料ティッシュ

こぼしちゃった
I spilled.

In Japan, people are quick to use tissue.
日本では割とすぐにティッシュを使う。

Japan has soft facial tissues, so blowing one's nose with a handkerchief is unthinkable!
鼻かみ用のやわらかいティッシュすら売っている日本で、ハンカチで鼻をかむのは、考えられない！！

チーン
ブブブ

えっ!?
うそ!
Huh?!
No way!

うわあ.
ちょっと待って
Hold on, there.

You don't even have to buy pocket tissues. Lots of tissues with ad inserts are handed out on the street.
ポケットティッシュは買わなくても、街を歩けば広告入りのを大量に配ってる。

ハイ
Here you go.

But you can't do this.
でも、これはダメよ。

そのティッシュ
ここに全部入れて
Hey, put all of those tissues in here.

Making full use of convenience stores

メイキング フゥ ユース オヴ
コンヴィーニエンス ストァーズ

コンビニを使いこなそう
Konbini o tsukaikonasoo

I'd like to pay my ○○.
アイド ライク トゥ ペイ マイ ○○

○○を支払いたいのですが
○○ o shiharaitai no desu ga.

utility bill
ユーティリティ ビゥ

公共料金
kookyoo ryookin

National Pension premium
ナショナゥ ペンション プリーミアム

国民年金保険料
kokumin nenkin hokenryoo

I'd like to send this by courier.
アイド ライク トゥ センド ズィス バイ クリアァ

これを宅配便で送りたいのですが
Kore o takuhaibin de okuritai no desu ga.

Please fill out this payment slip.
プリーズ フィゥ アウト ズィス ペイメント スリップ

こちらの伝票にご記入ください
Kochira no dempyoo ni gokinyuu kudasai.

> **COLUMN**
> Convenience store payment
> At most convenience stores, you can pay not only for utilities but also for items ordered from mail order companies, and as well as National Pension and National Health Insurance premiums and municipal and property taxes.
>
> コンビニで払えるもの
> 多くのコンビニのレジでは、各種公共料金のほか、主な通販会社での購入代金、国民年金保険料や国民健康保険料、さらには住民税や固定資産税などの税金までもが支払える。

Would you like to have your box lunch heated?
ウジュ ライク トゥ ハヴ ユアァ バクス ランチ ヒーティド↑

お弁当を温めますか？
Obentoo o atatamemasu ka?

Yes, please.
イェス プリーズ

お願いします
Onegaishimasu.

> **COLUMN**
> Convenience store pick-up
> Some online stores allow you to pick up the products you order at convenience stores. This service, which enables you to pick up items at any time, is popular among people who are busy during the day.
>
> コンビニ受け取り
> いくつかのインターネットの通販会社では、注文した商品をコンビニで受け取ることができるサービスをしている。24時間商品の受け取りが可能になるため、日中忙しい人などに人気のサービスだ。

I'd like to pick up the product I ordered.
アイド ライク トゥ ピック アップ ザ プラダクト アイ オーァダァド

注文した商品を受け取りたいのですが
Chuumonshita shoohin o uketoritai no desu ga.

Do you have the order number?
ドゥ ユ ハヴ ズィ オーァダァ ナンバァ↑

注文番号はお持ちですか？
Chuumonbangoo wa omochidesu ka?

★Many convenience stores also accept various types of e-money including Suica (see p. 21) and Edy (cell phone payment). Edy（おサイフケータイ）やSuica（P.21参照）などの電子マネーで支払できるコンビニも

photo print
フォウトウ　プリント
写真プリント
shashin purinto

gift order
ギフト　オーァダァ
ギフトの注文
gifuto no chuumon

Nearly all convenience stores have catalogs for ordering seasonal gifts and other types of presents.

ほとんどのコンビニでは、時節の贈り物など、さまざまなギフトを注文できるカタログを用意している。

---

alcohol
アゥカホゥ
酒類
sakerui

food
フード
食品
shokuhin

DVD
ディーヴィーディー
DVD
diibuidii

video games
ヴィディオウ　ゲイムズ
ゲーム
geemu

precooked dishes
プリクックト　ディッシィズ
惣菜
soozai

cigarettes
スィガレッツ
タバコ
tabako

snacks
スナックス
お菓子
okashi

daily goods
デイリィ　グッズ
日用品
nichiyoohin

microwave
マイクロウェイヴ
電子レンジ
denshirenji

stationery
ステイショナリィ
文房具
bunboogu

postcard
ポウストカード
ハガキ
hagaki

pot
パット
ポット
potto

ATM
エイティーエム
ATM
eetiiemu

book
ブック
本
hon

stamp
スタンプ
切手
kitte

newspapers
ニューズペイパァズ
新聞
shimbun

magazines
マガズィーンズ
雑誌
zasshi

ticket purchase terminal
ティケット　パーァチェス　ターァミナゥ
チケット購入端末
chiketto koonyuu tammatsu

FAX machine
ファクス　マシーン
FAX
fakkusu

copy machine
コゥピィ　マシーン
コピー機
kopiiki

●ATM　ATM

Nearly all convenience stores have ATMs. A transaction fee is usually incurred, but there are banks that offer savings accounts with "no transaction fees" as a benefit.

ほとんどのコンビニにはATMが設置されている。通常手数料がかかるが、手数料無料の特典の付いた普通預金口座を用意している銀行もある。

●Ticket purchase terminal　チケット購入端末

Many convenience stores have terminals that allow you to pay for and pick up tickets for movie, concert, and travel bookings. Some terminals also allow you to make reservations.

予約済みの映画やコンサート、旅行などのチケットの支払い・受け取りのできる端末が置いてあるコンビニが多い。なかにはチケット予約のできる端末もある。

★ Nearly all convenience stores, restaurants, and chain stores offer "point cards" that allow customers to use "points" for shopping. ほとんどのコンビニや飲食店、チェーン店などに、ポイントを買物に使えるポイントカードがある

Using fleamarkets and thrift shops

ユーズィング フリーマーァケット
アンド スリフト シャプス

フリーマーケット・リサイクルショップを利用しよう
Furiimaaketto, risaikuru shoppu o riyoo shiyoo

はじめよう / 歩こう / 買おう / 食べよう / 暮らそう / 伝えよう / 知っておこう

Could you lower the price a little?
クジュ ロウァァ ザ プライス ア リトゥ↑

もう少し安くしてもらえませんか？

Moosukoshi yasukushite moraemasen ka?

How about two for ~ yen?
ハウ アバウト トゥー フォア ～ イェン

2つで～円にしてもらえませんか？

Futatsu de ~ en nishite moraemasen ka?

COLUMN

Selling items at flea markets
Information about flea markets can be found in local PR bulletins and other newsletters. You can also apply for flea markets throughout the country via the website of the host organization.

フリーマーケットへの出店
自治体の広報誌などにはフリーマーケットの開催・出店募集の情報が掲載されている。また、主なフリーマーケット主催団体のサイトでは、全国各地のフリーマーケットへの出店申し込みができるようになっている。

● **Fleamarket** フリーマーケット

clothing クロウズィング 衣類 irui

daily goods デイリィ グッズ 日用品 nichiyoohin

antiques アンティークス 骨董品 kottoohin

toys トイズ オモチャ omocha

How old is this?
ハウ オウゥド イズ ズィス

これはいつ頃のものですか？

Kore wa itsugoro no mono desu ka?

thrift shop
スリフト シャプ

リサイクルショップ

risaikuru shoppu

Some large-scale shops deal in everything from electric appliances and furniture to brand-name items and clothing, while others specialize in buying unwanted items.

電化製品や家具、ブランド品、衣料まで多様な商品を扱う大型の総合リサイクル店や、買取り専門店などがある。

vintage clothing shop
ヴィンティジ クロウズィング シャプ

古着屋

furugiya

used goods
ユーズド グッズ

中古品

chuukohin

antique fair
アンティーク フェアァ

骨董市

kotto ichi

At antique fairs, you'll find a wide range of items, from vintage antiques and artifacts to bric-a-brac. They are often held on the grounds of shrines and temples.

骨董市には希少価値のある古美術や古道具からガラクタまで、さまざまなものが並ぶ。神社仏閣の境内で開かれることが多い。

unused stock
アニューズド スタック

新古品

shinkohin

★Flea markets are often referred to as *"furima."*
フリーマーケットは略して「フリマ」と呼ばれることが多い

I'd like to sell this PC.
アイド ライク トゥ セゥ ズィス ピースィー

パソコンの買い取りをお願いします
Pasokon no kaitori o onegaishimasu.

video game software
ヴィディオウ ゲイム ソフトウェアァ

ゲームソフト
geemu sofuto

used books
ユーズド ブクス

古本
furuhon

children's clothes
チゥドレンズ クロウズ

子供服
kodomofuku

COLUMN

Electronics makers collect PCs and other appliances at a cost, whereas some recycling businesses will buy or take broken PCs and other items free of charge.

メーカーによるパソコンなど電化製品の自主回収もあるが、通常有料になっている。一方リサイクル業者の中には、故障品のパソコンなどの無料引き取り・買い取りを行っているところがあるので、チェックしてみよう。

free take-away
フリー テイカウェイ

無料引き取り
muryoo hikitori

It's unused, so could you give me a better price?
イッツ アニューズド ソウ クジュ ギヴ ミ ア ベタァ プライス↑

未使用なのでもう少し高くなりませんか？
Mishiyoonanode moosukoshi takaku narimasen ka?

I can't pay any more.
アイ キャント ペイ エニィ モアァ

これ以上は出せませんね
Koreijoo wa dasemasen ne.

brand-name item
ブランドネイム アイテム

ブランド品
burandohin

pawn shop
ポーン ショップ

質屋
shichiya

"*Shichiya*" are places that offer monetary loans for pawned items (collateral). Nowadays, instead of granting loans, pawn shops mostly buy and sell jewelry and brand-name items.

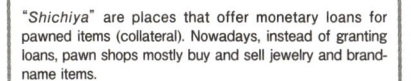

物品を質（担保）に取って、金銭を貸し付ける店を「質屋」という。現在では、金銭の貸し付けよりも、貴金属やブランド品などの買取や、質流れ品の販売などが中心になっている店が多い。

discount ticket shop
ディスカウント ティケット シャップ

金券ショップ
kinken shoppu

These shops buy various coupons, travel tickets, shareholder gift certificates, postcards, stamps, etc. and sell them at discount prices. They also sell railway book tickets individually.

「金券ショップ」では、さまざまな商品券や旅行券、株主優待券、またハガキや切手などを買い取り、通常より割安で販売している。ほかに、鉄道の回数券のバラ売りなどもしている。

★There are also convenience stores that sell nearly all of their merchandise—including perishable foods—for around 100 yen. 生鮮食品なども含めたほとんどの品を100円前後で売るコンビニもある

Tokyo's specialized shopping districts

トウキョウズ スペシャライズド
シャピング ディストリクツ
東京の専門店街
Tookyoo no senmontengai

I'm thinking of buying a snowboard.
アイム スィンキング オヴ バイング ア スノウボード
スノーボードを買おうと思ってるんだ
Sunooboodo o kaooto omotterunda.

In that case, you should go to Kanda.
Kanda has lots of sporting goods shops.
イン ザット ケイス ユ シュド ゴウ トゥ カンダ
カンダ ハズ ラッツ オヴ スポーティング グッズ シャプス
じゃあ神田に行ったらどう？
スポーツ用品店がたくさんあるよ
Jaa Kanda ni ittara doo?
Supootsuyoohinten ga takusan aruyo.

＊Numbers indicate the stations nearest each district.
各エリアへの最寄り駅を合番とした

Nishi-Ogikubo
Nishi-Ogikubo
❶西荻窪
Nishiogikubo

The Nishi-Ogikubo Station area, called "Antique Town," has as many as 60 stores selling antiques, sundries, vintage clothing, and recycled goods.

西荻窪駅周辺には、骨董品、古着、リサイクル店などが60ほど点在。「アンティーク街」「骨董街」とよばれる。

Nishi-Shinjuku
Nishi-Shinjuku
❷西新宿
Nishishinjuku

The streets running from the west exit of Shinjuku towards Okubo are lined with numerous record and CD shops for hardcore music fans.

新宿駅の西口から大久保方面にかけて、マニアックな音楽ファン向けのCD、中古レコードなどを揃えたショップが多数立ち並んでいる。

Ura-Harajuku
Ura-Harajuku
❸裏原宿
Uraharajuku

With "Cat Street" as the main thoroughfare, this area has many clothing and accessory shops targeting people in their teens and twenties.

「キャットストリート」を中心に、多くのブティックが店を構えている。10代、20代の若者を対象とした店が多い。

Nippori
Nippori
❹日暮里
Nippori

Called "Nippori Textile Town," this area has as many as 90 shops selling fabrics and handicraft goods at low prices.

駅南口の日暮里中央通りを中心に「日暮里繊維街」と呼ばれ、格安の生地やさまざまな手芸用品、服飾用品などを扱った店が90店ほどある。

Okachimachi
Okachimachi
❺御徒町
Okachimachi

Station map:
- ❶ Nishi-Ogikubo STN. 西荻窪駅
- ❷ Shinjuku STN. 新宿駅
- ❸ Harajuku STN. 原宿駅
- ❺ Okachimachi STN. 御徒町駅
- Sugamo STN. 巣鴨駅
- Otsuka STN. 大塚駅
- Ikebukuro STN. 池袋駅
- Mejiro STN. 目白駅
- Takadanobaba STN. 高田馬場駅
- Shin Okubo STN. 新大久保駅
- Yotsuya STN. 四ツ谷駅
- Yoyogi STN. 代々木駅
- Akasaka-mitsuke STN. 赤坂見附駅
- Omote-sando STN. 表参道駅
- Shibuya STN. 渋谷駅
- Ebisu STN. 恵比寿駅
- Meguro STN. 目黒駅
- Gotanda STN. 五反田駅
- Osaki STN. 大崎駅
- JR Yamanote Line JR山手線

LEGEND 凡例
- JR Lines JR路線
- Ginza Line 東京メトロ銀座線

★ "Ameyoko," a market in Tokyo's Ueno lined with stores selling fish and dry foods as well as miscellaneous goods, is a popular tourist spot. 魚介類や乾物、雑貨などの店が並ぶアメ横は、観光客にも人気

Where should I go to buy ○○?
ウェァァ シュド アイ ゴウ トゥ バイ ○○

○○を買うにはどの街に行ったらいい?
○○ o kauniwa dono machi ni ittara ii?

East Ueno
East Ueno

❻ 東上野

Higashiueno

Lined with Korean restaurants and grocery stores, the oldest "Korean town" in Tokyo is also referred to as "Kimchi alley."

焼肉店などの韓国料理店や食材店が軒を連ねる、都内最古の「リトルコリアンタウン」。「キムチ横丁」ともよばれている。

Kappabashi
Kappabashi

❼ 合羽橋

Kappabashi

Known as "Kitchen Town," you'll find over 170 stores selling cutlery, cookware, and food samples. Note that many stores are closed on Sundays and holidays.

「かっぱ橋道具街」には、食器や調理器具、食品サンプルの店が170店以上。日曜・祝日は多くが休み。

Akihabara
Akihabara

❽ 秋葉原

Akihabara

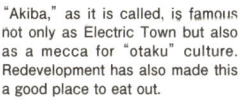

"Akiba," as it is called, is famous not only as Electric Town but also as a mecca for "otaku" culture. Redevelopment has also made this a good place to eat out.

「アキバ」の略称で呼ばれる。電気街だけでなく、フィギュアなどオタク文化のメッカとしても有名。近年は再開発により飲食店も充実。

Asakusabashi
Asakusabashi

❾ 浅草橋

Asakusabashi

Referred to as "Beads Town," the area around Asakusabashi Station has as many as 50 shops selling beads, natural rocks and other beadwork accessories.

浅草橋駅周辺には、多様なビーズ、天然石、ビーズ手芸用具の店が50店ほどあり、「ビーズタウン」とよばれている。

Kanda Jimbocho
Kanda Jimbocho

❿ 神田神保町

Kanda jimboochoo

This "Book Town," with 170 used book shops and over 30 new book shops, also has many foreign specialized book stores, foreign book stores, and publishing houses.

古書店が170店、新刊書店が30店以上ある「本の街」。専門書店、洋書店、また出版社も多い。

Kanda Ogawamachi
Kanda Ogawamachi

⓫ 神田小川町

Kanda ogawamachi

Has nearly 50 sporting goods shops, mostly along Yasukuni Street. In the area from Ogawamachi to Ochanomizu, you'll also find many musical instrument shops.

主に靖国通り沿いに、スポーツ用品店が50店近く立ち並ぶ。小川町から御茶ノ水にかけては楽器店も多い。

Okachimachi, most famous for "Ameyoko," is also the home of many jewelry shops and wholesalers. With over 100 jewelry shops, it's a good place to look for low-priced jewelry.

アメ横で有名な御徒町だが、宝飾専門店・問屋街もある。100店以上の宝飾品店では、割安なジュエリーが探せる。

That town is famous for ○○.
ザット タウン イズ フェイマス フォァ ○○

あの街は○○で有名なんですよ
Ano machi wa ○○ de yuumei nandesu yo.

★ Tokyo's Tsukiji is famous as the site of Japan's largest wholesale fish market. Despite a recent surge in tourists, the location may be moved. 東京の築地は日本最大の魚の卸売市場。近年一般客や観光客が急増。移転の予定も

43

Shopping streets

シャピング ストリーツ

商店街
Shootengai

Does this shopping street have a ○○?
ダズ ズィス シャピング ストリート ハヴ ア ○○↑

この商店街に○○はありますか？

Kono shootengai ni ○○ wa arimasu ka?

Can I buy just one of those?
キャナイ バイ ジャスト ワン オヴ ゾウズ↑

それはひとつでも買えますか？

Sore wa hitotsu demo kaemasu ka?

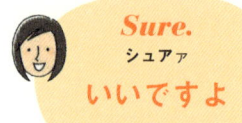

Sure.
シュアァ

いいですよ

Iidesu yo.

Sorry, it's three for 100 yen.
サリィ イッツ スリー フォア ワン ハンドレッド イェン

すいません、3つで100円です

Suimasen, mittsu de hyakuen desu.

If I buy ten, can you give me one for free?
イフ アイ バイ テン キャン ユ ギヴ ミ ワン フォア フリー↑

10個買うからひとつおまけしてくれる？

Jikko kaukara hitotsu omakeshite kureru?

arcade
アーァケイド

アーケード

aakeedo

meat shop ミート シャップ 肉屋 nikuya	**liquor shop** リカァ シャップ 酒屋 sakaya	**shoe shop** シュー シャップ 靴屋 kutsuya	**rice shop** ライス シャップ 米屋 komeya	**bakery** ベイカリィ パン屋 pan-ya
yakitori shop ヤキトウリィ シャップ 焼き鳥屋 yakitoriiya	**watch shop** ワッチ シャップ 時計屋 tokeiya	**coffee shop** カフィ シャップ 喫茶店 kissaten	**cleaner's** クリーナァズ クリーニング屋 kuriininguya	

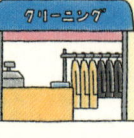

★One of the pleasures of shopping streets is walking around and enjoying foods, such as yakitori and bean cakes, that can be bought one at a time. 焼き鳥やおはぎなど、ひとつずつでも買える商店街では、食べ歩きも楽しい

Don't touch the merchandise!
ドゥント タッチ ザ マーチャンダイズ

品物に触んないでね！

Shinamono ni sawan-naide ne!

200 grams of ○○, please.
トゥー ハンドレッド グラムズ オヴ ○○ プリーズ

○○を200グラムください

○○ o nihyaku guramu kudasai.

COLUMN

As people come to use supermarkets and large shopping centers more and more for their daily shopping, many shopping streets have fallen into decline. However, since they also offer a nostalgic glimpse into the past, old shopping streets with names such as "○○ Ginza" are worth a visit.

日常の買物にスーパーや大型ショッピングセンターが使われるようになり、衰退している商店街も多い。しかし、昔ながらの商店街では懐かしい昭和の風景が見られるので、「○○銀座」と名の付いた商店街を覗いてみるのもいいだろう。

COLUMN

Shopping streets engaged in revitalization efforts offer point cards, seasonal sales, lotteries, festivals, parades and other local community-based events. Some shopping streets also offer shopping services for elderly people who have trouble doing their own daily shopping.

ポイントカードなどで活性化を図る商店街では、季節ごとのセール、福引のほか、お祭りやパレードなど、地域と一体となって開催されるイベントも楽しめる。また、日常の買物に困っている高齢者などのために買物代行サービスを行う商店街も出てきた。

Cut up the fish into three portions.
カット アップ ザ フィッシュ イントゥ スリー ポーションズ

魚を3枚におろしてください

Sakana o sammai ni oroshite kudasai.

I'd like to have a ○○ repaired.
アイド ライク トゥ ハヴ ア ○○ リペアァド

○○の修理をお願いします

○○ no shuuri o onegaishimasu.

---

fish shop フィッシュ シャップ 魚屋 sakanaya

clothing shop クロウズィング シャップ 衣料品店 iryoohinten

deli デリ 総菜屋 soozaiya

noodle shop ヌードゥ シャップ そば屋 sobaya

hardware shop ハードウェア シャップ 金物屋 kanamonoya

Japanese confectionery shop ジャパニーズ コンフェクショナリィ シャップ 和菓子屋 wagashiya

penny candy shop ペニィ キャンディ シャップ 駄菓子屋 dagashiya

optician オプティシャン 眼鏡屋 meganeya

greengrocer's グリーングロウサーズ 八百屋 yaoya

★ "Dagashiya," stores that sell cheap sweets and toys to children, have seen their numbers decline greatly in modern times. 「駄菓子屋」は子供を対象にした安価な菓子やおもちゃを売る店だが、現代ではずいぶん減少している

Buying daily sundries

バイング デイリィ サンドゥリィズ
生活雑貨を買おう
Seikatsu zakka o kaoo

Where can I buy ○○?
ウェアァ キャナイ バイ ○○
○○はどこで買えますか？
○○ wa dokode kaemasu ka?

Do you sell ○○?
ドゥ ユ セゥ ○○↑
○○は売っていますか？
○○ wa utte imasuka?

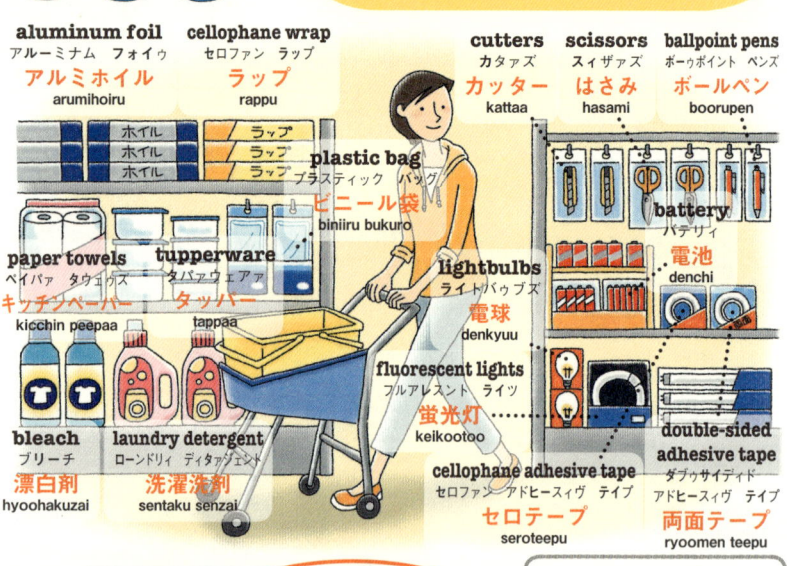

aluminum foil アルーミナム フォイゥ
アルミホイル arumihoiru

cellophane wrap セロファン ラップ
ラップ rappu

cutters カタァズ
カッター kattaa

scissors スィザァズ
はさみ hasami

ballpoint pens ボーゥポイント ペンズ
ボールペン boorupen

plastic bag プラスティック バッグ
ビニール袋 biniiru bukuro

paper towels ペイパァ タウェゥズ
キッチンペーパー kicchin peepaa

tupperware タパァウェアァ
タッパー tappaa

lightbulbs ライトバゥブズ
電球 denkyuu

battery バテリィ
電池 denchi

fluorescent lights フルアレスント ライツ
蛍光灯 keikootoo

bleach ブリーチ
漂白剤 hyoohakuzai

laundry detergent ローンドゥリィ ディタァジェンド
洗濯洗剤 sentaku senzai

cellophane adhesive tape セロファン アドヒースィヴ テイプ
セロテープ seroteepu

double-sided adhesive tape ダブゥサイディド アドヒースィヴ テイプ
両面テープ ryoomen teepu

WORDBANK DIY 日曜大工

English	Katakana	Japanese	Romaji
screwdriver	スクリュードライバァ	ドライバー	doraibaa
hammer	ハマァ	とんかち	tonkachi
screw	スクリュー	ねじ	neji
nail	ネイゥ	くぎ	kugi
pliers	プライアァズ	ペンチ	penchi
saw	ソー	のこぎり	nokogiri
stepladder	ステプラダァ	脚立	kyatatsu
paint	ペイント	ペンキ	penki
brush	ブラッシュ	はけ	hake

100 yen shop
ワン ハンドレッド イェン シャップ
100円ショップ
hyakuen shoppu

These shops sell a wide range of products for 100 yen. They are also referred to as "hyakkin," an abbreviation of "hyakuen kin-itsu (uniform price of 100 yen)."

多様な商品を原則として1点100均一で販売する。「100円均一」を略して「100均（ひゃっきん）」とも呼ばれる。

★In Japan, some people beat their futons in order to expel dust and ticks, but vacuuming them is just as effective. 日本ではホコリやダニを出そうと布団を叩く人がいるが、掃除機で直接吸うのが効果的

What is this used for?
ワット イズ ズィス ユーズド フォァ
これは何に使うんですか？
Kore wa nani ni tsukaundesu ka?

It's used to beat futons.
イッツ ユーズド トゥ ビート フトンズ
それで布団を叩くんですよ
Sore de futon o tatakundesu yo.

futon clip
フトン クリップ
布団ばさみ
futon basami

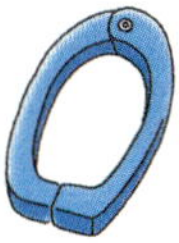

mosquito net
モスキートウ ネット
蚊帳
kaya

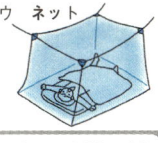

Nets hung from the ceiling for repelling mosquitoes and other pests, they are no longer very common, but have attracted renewed interest as an insecticide-free form of pest control.
天井から吊るす、蚊などの害虫除けの網。最近はあまり使われないが、殺虫剤を使わないため見直されている。

mosquito coil
モスキートウ コイゥ
蚊取り線香
katorisenkoo

Fumigant-type insecticide with pyrethrum and other insect-repelling ingredients kneaded into incense. They are usually coil-shaped and green in color.
主に蚊を駆除する目的で、線香に除虫菊などの有効成分を練り込んだ、燻煙式殺虫剤。緑色の渦巻き型が多い。

duster
ダスタァ
はたき
hataki

toilet seat cover
トイレット スィート カヴァァ
便座カバー
benza kabaa

Relatively uncommon in the West, around half of all Japanese households use toilet seat covers. Toilet floor mats are also common.
欧米では使う人が限られているが、日本では半数程度の人が便座カバーを使用していると言われる。トイレの床マットも一般的。

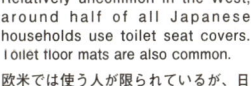

laundry net
ローンドリィ ネット
洗濯用ネット
sentakuyoo netto

earpick
イァァピック
耳かき
mimikaki

Japanese ear picks are typically made of bamboo and have ladle-shaped tips. Many Japanese favor these ear picks because their ear wax tends to be dry.
日本の一般的な耳かきは竹製で先端がヘラ状。多くの日本人の耳垢は乾燥しており、このような耳かきが好まれる。

lint filter
リント フィゥタァ
糸くずフィルター
itokuzu firutaa

laundry hanger
ローンドリィ ハンガァ
物干しハンガー
monohoshi hangaa

Hangers with dozens of clothespins attached to them and "octopus leg"-type hangers are popular because they allow one to hang out large amounts of laundry in a small space.
狭いスペースに効率よく洗濯物を干すため、洗濯ばさみが数十個付いたものやタコ足型のハンガーが人気だ。

drain cleaner
ドレイン クリーナァ
排水溝クリーナー
haisuikoo kuriinaa

★In recent years, it has become more common to use electric devices instead of mosquito coils.
最近は、渦巻きの蚊取り線香に代わって、電気を使った器具が主流になっている

Drugstore
ドラッグストーァ
ドラッグストア
Doraggu sutoa

Do you accept prescriptions?
ドゥ ユ アクセプト プリスクリプションズ↑
処方箋は受け付けてもらえますか？
Shohoosen wa uketsukete moraemasu ka?

Yes, we do.
イェス ウィ ドゥ
はい、承ります
Hai, uketamawarimasu.

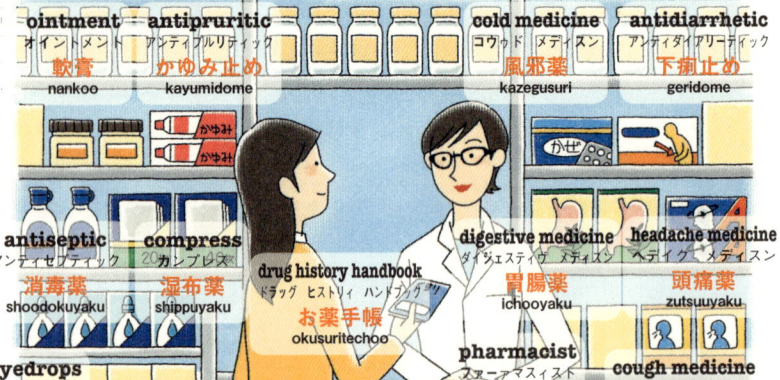

● **Pharmacy** 薬局

ointment オイントメント
軟膏 nankoo

antipruritic アンティプルリティック
かゆみ止め kayumidome

cold medicine コウッド メディスン
風邪薬 kazegusuri

antidiarrhetic アンティダイアリーティック
下痢止め geridome

antiseptic アンティセプティック
消毒薬 shoodokuyaku

compress カンプレス
湿布薬 shippuyaku

drug history handbook ドラッグ ヒストリィ ハンドブック
お薬手帳 okusuritechoo

digestive medicine ダイジェスティヴ メディスン
胃腸薬 ichooyaku

headache medicine ヘディク メディスン
頭痛薬 zutsuuyaku

eyedrops アイドラプス
目薬 megusuri

prescription statement プリスクリプション ステイトメント
処方明細書 shohoomeisaisho

pharmacist ファーマシスト
薬剤師 yakuzaishi

cough medicine コフ メディスン
咳止め sekidome

WORDBANK — Pharmaceuticals 医薬品

adhesive bandage
アドヒースィヴ バンデッジ
ばんそうこう
bansookoo

bandage
バンデッジ
包帯
hootai

motion sickness medicine モウション スィックネス メディスン
酔い止め yoidome

antipyretic アンティパイレティック
解熱剤 genetsuzai

nasal allergy medicine ネイズゥ アラジィ メディスン
鼻炎薬 bien-yaku

antibiotic アンティバイアティック
抗生物質 koosei busshitsu

suppository サパズィトリィ
坐薬 zayaku

painkiller ペインキラァ
鎮痛剤 chintsuuzai

tranquilizer トランキライザァ
精神安定剤 seishin-anteizai

sleeping medicine スリーピング メディスン
睡眠薬 suimin-yaku

★Drugstores in Japan mainly sell medicine, and do not necessarily sell sundries or foods. 日本のドラッグストアは元々は薬中心で、必ずしも雑貨や食べ物があるわけではない

insect repellent (for clothing)
インセクト リペラント
(衣類の) 防虫剤
(iruino) boochuuzai

wet tissue
ウェット ティシュー
ウエットティッシュ
uetto tisshu

feminine hygiene products
フェミニン ハイジーン プラダクツ
生理用品
seiriyoohin

contact lens solution
カンタクト レンズ ソルーション
コンタクト溶液
kontakuto yooeki

insecticide
インセクティサイド
殺虫剤
sacchuuzai

cleaner
クリーナ
洗剤
senzai

air freshener
エアァ フレシュナァ
芳香剤
hookoozai

tissue
ティシュー
ティッシュ
tisshu

baby food
ベイビィ フード
ベビーフード
bebiifuudo

toilet paper
トイレット ペイパァ
トイレットペーパー
toiretto peepaa

insect repellent spray
インセクト リペラント スプレイ
虫除けスプレー
mushiyoke supuree

dehumidifying agent
ディヒューミディファイング エイジェント
除湿剤
joshitsuzai

baby formula
ベイビィ フォーマュラ
粉ミルク
konamiruku

diapers
ダイパァズ
オムツ
omutsu

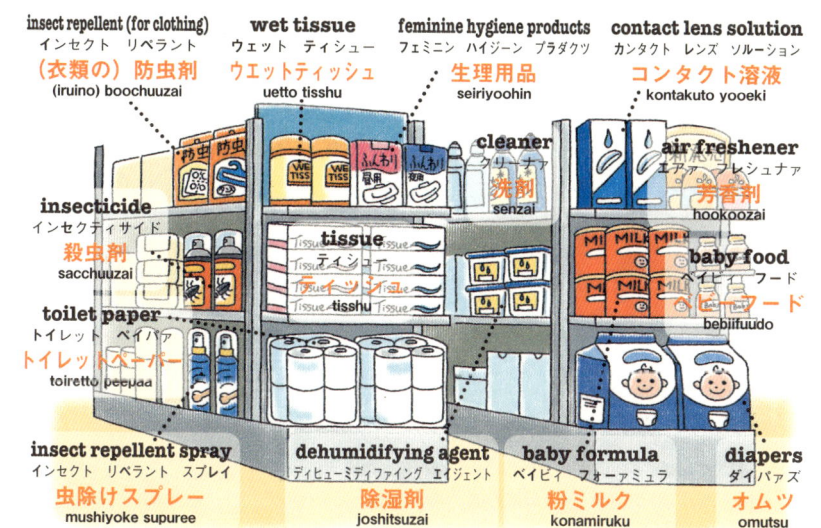

Which foundation / face wash is good for ○○?
ウィッチ ファウンデイション／フェイス ワッシュ イズ グッド フォア ○○
○○にはどのファンデーション/洗顔料がいいですか？
○○ ni wa dono fandeeshon / senganryoo ga iidesu ka?

---

dry skin
ドライ スキン
乾燥肌
kansoohada

sensitive skin
センスィティヴ スキン
敏感肌
binkanhada

oily skin
オイリィ スキン
脂性肌
aburashoohada

pimples
ピンプゥズ
ニキビ
nikibi

COLUMN

Some drugstores have prescription counters and some don't. Even places without a pharmacist are allowed to sell most pharmaceuticals as long as a "registered salesperson" is on hand. Drugstore cosmetic counters are popular with women for their low prices, large selection, and convenience.

ドラッグストアには処方箋を受け付ける薬局を併設したものとそうでないものがある。薬剤師がいない場合も、登録販売者がいれば大半の一般医薬品は売ってもらえる。ドラッグストアの化粧品売場は、安さや品揃え、自由に試せる気軽さが女性に受けている。

WORDBANK — Toiletries トイレタリー

English	カタカナ	日本語	romaji
face lotion	フェイス ロウション	化粧水	keshoosui
milky lotion	ミゥキィ ロウション	乳液	nyuueki
makeup remover	メイカップ リムーヴァァ	メイク落とし	meiku otoshi
hair dye	ヘアァ ダイ	ヘアカラー	hea karaa
depilatory	ディピラトリィ	脱毛剤	datsumoozai
hair growth stimulant	ヘアァ グロゥス スティミュラント	養毛剤	yoomoozai
bath additive	バス アディティヴ	入浴剤	nyuuyokuzai
razor	レイザァ	カミソリ	kamisori

★ Drugstores selling the latest cosmetics and confectioneries are also popular among high school girls and working women. 化粧品やお菓子など新製品が次々並ぶドラッグストアは、女子高生やOLなどにも大人気

Electrical appliances and furniture

イレクトリカゥ アプライアンスィズ アンド ファニチャァ

家電製品・家具
Kadenseihin, kagu

Which ○○ is selling well?
ウィッチ ○○ イズ セリング ウェゥ
売れ筋の○○はどれですか？
Uresuji no ○○ wa dore desuka?

This product is the most popular.
ズィス プラダクト イズ モゥスト パピュラァ
こちらの製品が一番人気です
Kochira no seihin ga ichiban ninki desu.

This is today's special.
ズィス イズ トゥデイズ スペシャゥ
今日の特売品はこちらです
Kyoo no tokubaihin wa kochira desu.

electrical appliance store
イレクトリカゥ アプライアンス ストァ
電器店
denkiten

air conditioner エアァ コンディショナァ エアコン eakon

bread maker ブレッド メイカァ ホームベーカリー hoomu beekarii

toaster トゥスタァ トースター toosutaa

dishwasher ディシュワシャァ 食器洗い機 shokki araiki

washing machine ワシング マシーン 洗濯機 sentakki

refrigerator リフリジェレイタァ 冷蔵庫 reizooko

microwave oven マイクロウェイヴ オヴン 電子レンジ denshi renji

TV ティーヴィー TV terebi

stereo ステリオゥ ステレオ sutereo

telephone テレフォゥン 電話機 denwaki

DVD player ディーヴィーディー プレイヤァ DVDプレーヤー diibuidii pureeyaa

rice cooker ライス クカァ 炊飯器 suihanki

cell phone セゥ フォゥン ケータイ keitai

computer コンピュータァ パソコン pasokon

iron アイアン アイロン airon

vacuum cleaner ヴァキューム クリーナァ 掃除機 soojiki

★Since electrical appliances such as rice cookers, refrigerators, and washing machines are often white, they are called "shiromono" (white) appliances. 炊飯器、冷蔵庫、洗濯機などの電化製品は、「白物家電」と呼ばれる

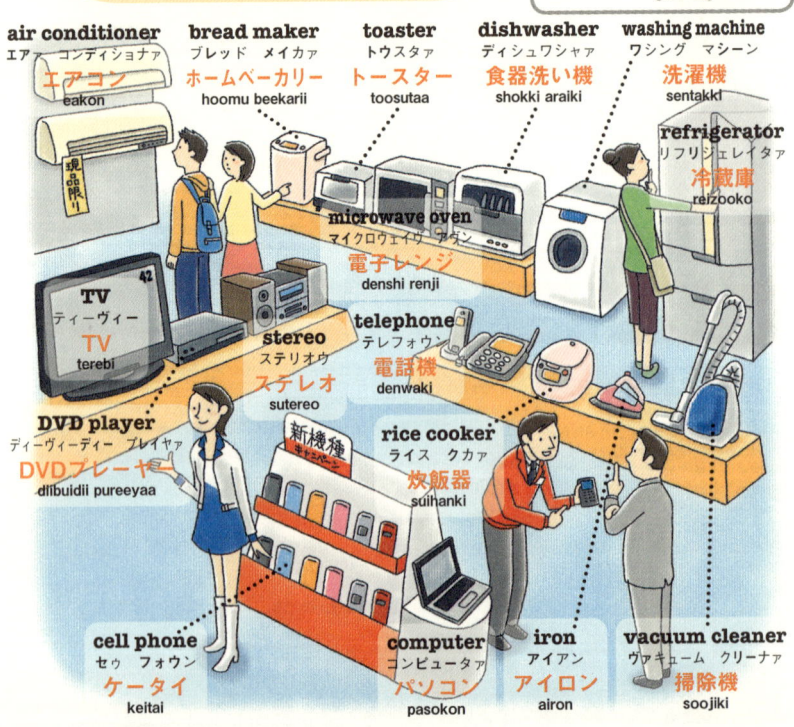

Can you install the air conditioner for me?
キャン ユ インストーゥ ズィ エァア コンディショナァ フォア ミ↑

エアコンの取り付けをお願いします

Eakon no toritsuke o onegaishimasu.

installation fee
インスタレイション フィー

設置料

secchiryoo

Please send it by ~.
プリーズ センド イット バイ ~

~までに配送してください

~ made ni haisooshite kudasai.

delivery charge
デリヴァリィ チャーァジ

配送料

haisooryoo

trade-in
トレイドイン

下取り

shitadori

Please fill out this delivery slip.
プリーズ フィゥ アウト ズィス デリヴァリィ スリップ

こちらの配送伝票に記入してください

Kochira no haisoodempyoo ni kinyuushite kudasai.

WORDBANK — Health appliances 健康家電

English	カタカナ	日本語	romaji
air cleaner	エアァア クリーナァ	空気清浄機	kuukiseijooki
humidifier	ヒューミディファイアァ	加湿機	kashitsuki
futon dryer	フトン ドライヤァ	布団乾燥機	futon kansooki
massager	マサージャア	マッサージ機	massaajiki
water purifier	ウォータァ ピュリファイアァ	浄水機	joosuiki
hair dryer	ヘアァ ドライヤァ	ヘアドライヤー	hea doraiyaa
electric shaver	エレクトリック シェイヴァァ	シェーバー	sheebaa
electric toothbrush	エレクトリック トゥースブラッシュ	電動歯ブラシ	dendoo haburashi

order
オーァダァ

注文する

chuumonsuru

order (an item not in stock)
オーァダァ

取り寄せする

toriyose suru

furniture store
ファァニチャァ ストーァ

家具店

kaguten

assembly
アセンブリィ

組み立て

kumitate

WORDBANK — Furniture 家具

bed	ベッド	ベッド	beddo
sofa	ソウファ	ソファ	sofa
table	テイブゥ	テーブル	teeburu
chair	チェアァ	イス	isu
sideboard	サイドボーァド	サイドボード	saidoboodo
storage shelf	ストーリッジ シェゥ	収納棚	shuunoodana
cupboard	カバーァド	食器棚	shokkidana
TV stand	ティーヴィー スタンド	AVラック	eebui rakku
curtains	カーァテンズ	カーテン	kaaten

★Nearly all mass retailers of electrical appliances offer a "point card" for accumulating points that can be used for payment at the store. ほとんどの家電量販店では、購入時のポイントが支払い時に使えるポイントカードがある

Being a smart shopper

ビーイング ア スマーァト シャパァ
お得に買物しよう
Otokuni kaimono shiyoo

When does the bargain sale start?
ウェン ダズ ザ バーァゲン セイウ スタート
バーゲンセールはいつからですか？
Baagen seeru wa itsukara desu ka?

What is the discount on this?
ワット イズ ザ ディスカウント オン ズィス
これは何割引きですか？
Kore wa nanwaribiki desu ka?

This is 40% off.
ズィス イズ フォーァティ パーァセント オフ
40％オフになっております
Yonjippaasento ofu ni natteorimasu.

---

lottery
ラタリィ
福引
fukubiki

Fukubiki involves drawing a ticket and collecting a prize if a "winner" is drawn. *Fukubiki* for sales promotions often involve the use of a "*garapon*."

くじをひき、当たった場合は景品等がもらえるのが福引。販売促進の一環でくじ引きには「ガラポン」と呼ばれる器具を用いることが多い。

lottery wheel
ラタリィ ウィーゥ
ガラポン
garapon

grab bag
グラブ バッグ
福袋
fukubukuro

Grab bags mainly sold at New Year's. Though cheaper than the total price of the contents, you usually don't know what's inside until you open it.

主にお正月時期に販売される、複数の商品が袋詰めになったもの。商品の合計金額より格安な値段だが、通常中身は開けてみるまでわからない。

time service
タイム サーァヴィス
タイムサービス
taimu saabisu

Limited-time discount sales. Supermarkets often offer discounts on precooked dishes and perishables in the evening.

時間限定の特売セールのこと。スーパーの夕方のタイムサービスでは、惣菜や生鮮食品が割引されることが多い。

Pre-cooked dishes are now 20% off.
プリクックト ディシィズ アァ ナウ トゥエンティ パーァセント オフ
これよりお惣菜全品2割引きです
Kore yori osoozai zempin niwaribiki desu.

These are not sale items.
ズィーズ アァ ナット セイウ アイテムズ
こちらはセール対象外です
Kochira wa seeru taishoogai desu.

はじめよう / 歩こう / 買おう / 食べよう / 暮らそう / 伝えよう / 知っておこう

★Japan normally has two sales seasons, in January and July. Seasonal products have been sold early at these sales recently. セールは、通常1月初旬からと7月初旬から。最近は季節商品が早めにバーゲンに出ることも

Is there a discount for cash payment?
イズ ゼアラ ア ディスカウント フォア キャッシュ ペイメント↑

現金割引はありますか

Genkin waribiki wa arimasu ka?

cash refund
キャッシュ リファンド

現金還元

genkin kangen

Some supermarkets and electronic stores implement special sales in which a certain percentage of the purchase amount is returned to the shopper on the spot.

買上げ金額の一定の割合を、その場で現金還元するという特別セールを実施するスーパーや家電量販店もある。

point refund
ポイント リファンド

ポイント還元

pointo kangen

System in which a certain percentage of the amount spent is kept as "points" that can be used for shopping. You can usually get more points by paying in cash.

買上げ金額の一定の割合で付くポイントを買物に使えるシステム。現金払いでポイント還元率が上がる。

Today is double-point day!
トゥデイ イズ ダブゥポイント デイ

今日はポイント2倍デーです！

Kyoo wa pointo nibai dee desu!

Supermarkets, electronic stores, and online shops sometimes have campaigns in which they offer more points than usual for a limited time.

スーパーや家電量販店、またネットショップなどでも、ポイント還元の割合を通常より上げるキャンペーンを実施していることがある。

COLUMN
Getting discount coupons
Many of the free newsletters at storefronts and train stations have coupons that can be used to get discounts and other privileges at places such as restaurants and hairdressers. Many coupons are also available online.

お得なクーポン入手法
駅構内や店先には、飲食店や美容院で使える、割引などの特典の付いたクーポン中心のフリーマガジンが置いてあるのでチェックしてみよう。またインターネットサイトからダウンロードできるクーポンも多数ある。

Can I use this coupon?
キャナイ ユーズ ズィス クーポン↑

このクーポンは使えますか？

Kono kuupon wa tsukaemasu ka?

outlet mall
アウトレット モーゥ

アウトレットモール

autoretto mooru

There are more than 30 outlet malls nationwide selling items from famous makers and brands at low prices. They are mainly located in the suburbs or at tourist spots.

メーカー品、ブランド品を格安で買えるアウトレットモールは、全国に30カ所以上ある。主に郊外や観光地に立地する。

unredeemed article sales
アンリディームド アーァティクゥ セイゥズ

質流れバーゲン

shichinagare baagen

Pawned items that went unredeemed are sold at low prices at "shichi nagare" sales. Put on by pawnbroker associations, they attract many customers.

金銭が返済されなかった質（担保）を格安で売る。地域の質屋組合が主催するもので、多くの客が集まる。

COLUMN
Duty-free shops in Japan
Duty-free shops that offer consumer tax exemptions exclusively to foreign travelers and Japanese living abroad can be found not only at airports but also places such as Akihabara. Some department stores also offer duty exemption services.

日本の免税店
短期滞在の外国人旅行者や海外居住の日本人が国外に持ち出す場合に限り、消費税がオフになる免税店は、空港以外にも秋葉原などにある。免税手続きができるデパートもあるので問い合せてみよう。

Can you fill out my duty-exemption forms here?
キャン ユ フィゥ アウト マイ デューティィ イグゼンプション フォーァムズ ヒアァ↑

免税手続きはできますか？

Menzei tetsuzuki wa dekimasu ka?

★ Department stores often have a special area—commonly on the basement or top floor—where items are sold at bargain prices all year round. デパートでは、地下や最上階の特設会場で年中何らかのセールをしている

Getting a Bite
食べよう

Natto 納豆

The no. 1 Japanese food that foreigners can't eat!
外国人が食べられない日本の食べ物第一位！！

That smell, and that stickiness… Yuck!
まず匂いがダメ、ネバネバがダメ。

If you put it in curry, it's neither smelly nor sticky. …Then again, maybe you don't need to eat it in the first place.
カレーに入れると匂いもネバネバも消える…というが、そうまでして食べなくてもいい…かも。

スプーンで食べればネバネバでも大丈夫！
If you eat it with a spoon, the stickiness is no problem!

No!!

Fractionalization 細分化

In Japan, a single product comes in many different types. Take coffee, for example.
日本では、ひとつの商品でもさまざまな種類がある。例えば缶コーヒー。

どれにしよう？
Which one should I get?

工夫の国・日本！
Japan, land of ingenuity!

- ブラック black
- 深煎 deep-roasted
- 微糖 lightly sweetened
- ミルク入リ with milk
- 砂糖ミルク入 with milk and sugar
- アメリカン American-style
- カフェオレ café au lait

Local ramens are also popular.
ご当地ラーメンも人気。

- 背脂 back fat
- みそ miso / 札幌 Sapporo
- 博多 Hakata
- 尾道 Onomichi
- 喜多方 Kitakata
- とんこつ pig bone
- 煮干 dried sardines

うまいよ Try some!

Before Valentine's Day, there's a surge in the variety of chocolate.
バレンタインデーになると、チョコの種類も拍車がかかる。

こんなチョコいらニャい～
Who needs these kinds of chocolate?

- いも虫チョコ caterpillar chocolate
- チョコ納豆 chocolate natto
- カニチョコ crab chocolate
- いかチョコ squid chocolate

Eating out

イーティング アウト
外食を楽しもう
Gaishoku o tanoshimoo

Wanna go get something to eat?
ワナ ゴウ ゲット サムスィング トゥ イート↑
一緒に食事に行かない？
Issho ni shokuji ni ikanai?

What kind of food do you like?
ワット カインド オヴ フード ドゥ ユ ライク
どんな料理が好き？
Donna ryoori ga suki?

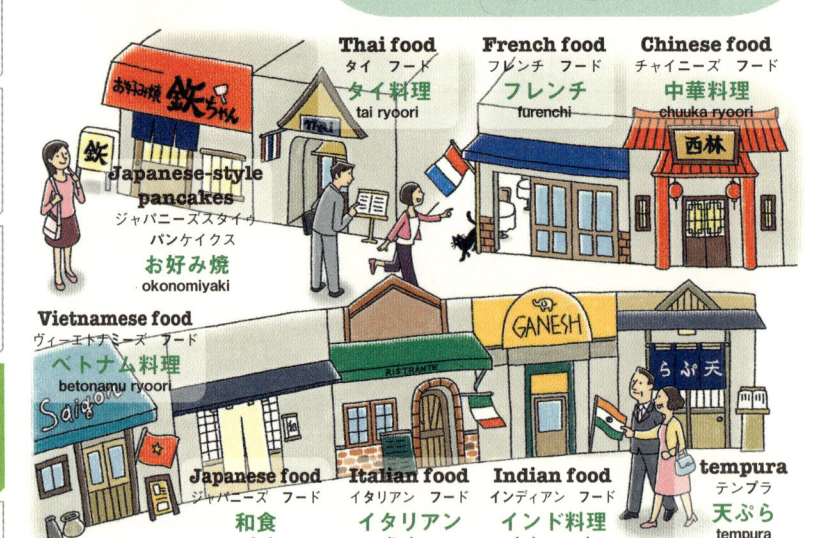

Thai food
タイ フード
タイ料理
tai ryoori

French food
フレンチ フード
フレンチ
furenchi

Chinese food
チャイニーズ フード
中華料理
chuuka ryoori

Japanese-style pancakes
ジャパニーズ スタイゥ パンケイクス
お好み焼
okonomiyaki

Vietnamese food
ヴィエトナミーズ フード
ベトナム料理
betonamu ryoori

Japanese food
ジャパニーズ フード
和食
washoku

Italian food
イタリアン フード
イタリアン
itarian

Indian food
インディアン フード
インド料理
indo ryoori

tempura
テンプラ
天ぷら
tempura

---

shabu-shabu
シャブシャブ
しゃぶしゃぶ
shabushabu

Thinly-sliced beef warmed briefly in a boiling pot and dipped in sesame or citrus sauce. Pork or fish can also be used.

薄切りの牛肉を、鍋で煮立っただし汁にくぐらせさっと火を通し、ゴマだれやポン酢につけて食べる。牛肉のほか、豚肉や白身の魚なども使う。

Korean-style grilled meat
コリアンスタイゥ グリゥド ミート
焼肉
yakiniku

"*Yakiniku*" restaurants serve Korean-style grilled meat (usually beef, but pork and chicken are also popular). You can also enjoy yakiniku at inexpensive chains.

「焼肉店」のほとんどが韓国風の焼肉を出す。牛肉中心だが最近は豚肉・鶏肉も人気。割安のチェーン店も。

full-course Japanese meal
フゥコーァス ジャパニーズ ミーゥ
会席料理
kaisekiryoori

Full-course Japanese meal in which seasonal ingredients are used, and close attention is paid to the ingredients' distinctive characteristics, as well as preparation method and presentation.

旬の素材を使い素材の持ち味を大切にした和食のコース料理。調理法、盛付けにも配慮している。

★"Viking," when used to refer to "all-you-can-eat" buffets, is Japlish. "Buffet" is also a commonly-used expression. 「バイキング」は和製英語、「ビュッフェ」という表現も一般的に使われている

Let's go to the hotel buffet.
レッツ ゴウ トゥ ザ ホテゥ バフェイ

ホテルのバイキングに行こうよ
Hoteru no baikingu ni ikooyo.

all-you-can-eat
オーゥ ユ キャン イート

食べ放題
tabehoodai

What kind of food do they have?
ワット カインド オヴ フード ドゥ ゼイ ハヴ

どんな食べ物があるの？
Donna tabemono ga aru no?

time limit
タイム リミット

時間制限
jikanseigen

COLUMN
Handling the bill
A smart way to treat your guest is to pay the bill when he/she is in the restroom, or when you get up to go to the restroom yourself. If the other party pays, wait outside the restaurant while the bill is being paid, then ask what the amount was and make a show of wanting to pay.

会計時のマナー
自分がおごりたい場合は、相手がトイレに立っている間、または自分がトイレに立つ際に精算を済ませるといい。相手が支払うときは店の外で待ち、あとから金額を聞いて払う意志を示そう。

full-course meal
フゥコーァス ミーゥ

コース料理
koosu ryoori

fixed-price meal
フィクスト プライス ミーゥ

プリフィックス
prifikkusu

light meal
ライト ミーゥ

軽い食事
karui shokuji

family restaurant
ファミリィ レストラント

ファミリーレストラン
famirii resutoran

Low-priced chain restaurants offering a wide variety of dishes, their appeal lies in their child-friendliness. Referred to as "famiresu."

低価格、メニューが豊富なチェーン展開のレストラン。子供連れも行きやすい。ファミレスとよばれる。

I'm stuffed.
アイム スタフト

もうおなかいっぱいだなあ
Moo onaka ippai da naa.

It's my treat.
イッツ マイ トリート

ここは僕がおごるよ
Koko wa boku ga ogoru yo.

Let's split the bill.
レッツ スプリット ザ ビゥ

割り勘にしよう
Warikan ni shiyoo.

Well, if you insist. Thank you for your kind offer.
ウェゥ イフ ユ インスィスト サンキュ フォア ユアァ カインド オファァ

じゃあお言葉に甘えて、ごちそうさまでした
Jaa okotoba ni amaete, gochisoosama deshita.

★ "Gochisōsama" is not just something you say after finishing a meal; it is also used to express thanks to a person who treats you. 「ごちそうさま」は食後のあいさつとしてだけでなく、食事をおごってくれた人にも言う

Restaurant talk

レストラント トーク
飲食店でのやり取り
Inshokuten de no yaritori

Welcome. How many in your party?
ウェゥカム ハウ メニィ イン ユアァ パーァティィ
いらっしゃいませ。何名様ですか？
Irasshaimase. Nammei sama desu ka?

Four. We don't have a reservation.
フォーァ ウィ ドゥント ハヴ ア リザヴェイション
4名です。予約はしていません
Yommei desu. Yoyaku wa shite imasen.

I'm afraid there are no seats available at the moment.
アイム アフレイド ゼァァ アァ ノウ スィーツ アヴェイラブゥ アット ザ モウメント
あいにく満席となっております
Ainiku manseki to natte orimasu.

This way, sir/ma'am.
ズィス ウェイ サーァ／マーム
お席にご案内します
Oseki ni goannai shimasu.

How long is the wait?
ハウ ロング イズ ザ ウェイト
どのくらい待ちますか？
Donokurai machimasu ka?

table seat
テイブゥ スィート
テーブル席
teeburuseki

tatami room
タタミ ルーム
座敷
zashiki

sharing a table
シェアリング ア テイブゥ
相席
aiseki

counter
カウンタァ
カウンター
kauntaa

Would you prefer smoking?
ウジュ プリファァ スモウキング↑
おタバコはお吸いになられますか？
Otabako wa osui ni nararemasu ka?

non-smoking seat
ノンスモウキング スィート
禁煙席
kin-en seki

smoking seat
スモウキング スィート
喫煙席
kitsuen seki

private room
プライヴェット ルーム
個室
koshitsu

★Some restaurants in other countries allow customers to bring their own alcohol, but not in Japan.
海外ではアルコール類を持ち込める飲食店もあるが、日本ではあまりない

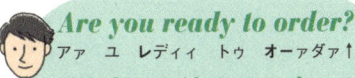

Are you ready to order?
ご注文はお決まりですか？
Gochuumon wa okimari desu ka?

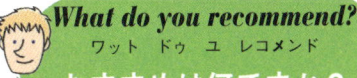

What do you recommend?
おすすめは何ですか？
Osusume wa nan desu ka?

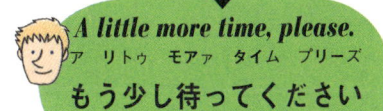

A little more time, please.
もう少し待ってください
Moo sukoshi matte kudasai.

Do you have an English menu?
英語のメニューはありますか？
Eigo no menyuu wa arimasu ka?

check
チェック
伝票
dempyoo

We're still waiting for our ○○.
○○がまだ来ていないのですが
○○ ga mada kiteinai no desu ga.

receipt
リスィート
領収書
ryooshuusho

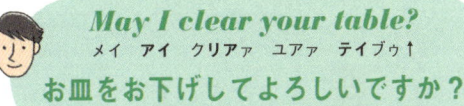

May I clear your table?
お皿をお下げしてよろしいですか？
Osara o osageshite yoroshiidesu ka?

Check, please.
お会計をお願いします
Okaikei o onegaishimasu.

Do you take credit cards?
クレジットカードは使えますか？
Kurejitto kaado wa tsukaemasu ka?

Can we pay separately?
別々に払っていいですか？
Betsubetsu ni haratte iidesu ka?

COLUMN

In Japan, the slip issued by cash registers is a "*reshiito*," whereas a "*ryōshusho*" is a receipt on which the addressee and other information can be entered, and is required by tax law. Some people have "Customer" written in the "addressee" blank instead of a name or company, but such receipts are not valid in tax inspections.

レジで発行するものを「レシート」、宛名やただし書きを入れるものを「領収書」というが、税法処理上では領収書が必要。宛名が名前や社名でなく「上様」では税務調査では認められない。

Please pay together.
まとめてお願いします
Matomete onegaishimasu.

★Tipping is not required at Japanese restaurants. Some places have a 10% service charge.
日本の飲食店では、チップは必要ない。10％程度のサービス料が課せられる店もある

Conveyor belt sushi bar

コンヴェイアァ ベゥト
スシ バーァ

回転寿司
Kaiten zushi

A plate of ○○, please.
ア プレイト オヴ ○○ プリーズ

○○一皿お願いします

○○ hitosara onegaishimasu.

○○, hold the wasabi, please.
○○ ホゥド ザ ワサビ プリーズ

○○をワサビ抜きでください

○○ o wasabi nuki de kudasai.

sushi formed by hand	rice (for sushi)	(sushi) topping	dried seaweed
スシ フォームド バイ ハンド	ライス（フォァ スシ）	（スシ）タピング	ドライド スィーウィード
握りずし	シャリ	ネタ	海苔
nigirizushi	shari	neta	nori

tuna	spotted shad	conger eel	salmon roe
チューナ	スパティド シャッド	カンガァ イーゥ	サモン ロウ
マグロ	コハダ	アナゴ	イクラ
maguro	kohada	anago	ikura

squid	octopus	shrimp	sea urchin
スクウィッド	アクトパス	シュリンプ	スィー アーァチン
イカ	タコ	エビ	ウニ
ika	tako	ebi	uni

WORDBANK — Sushi toppings 寿司ネタ

horse mackerel	ホーァス マカレゥ	アジ aji
salmon	サモン	サーモン saamon
ark shell	アーァク シェウ	赤貝 akagai
scallop	スカラップ	ホタテ hotate
sea bream	スィー ブリーム	鯛 tai
yellowtail	イェロウテイゥ	ハマチ hamachi
oily bluefin tuna	オイリィ ブルーフィン チューナ	トロ toro
flatfish	フラットフィッシュ	ヒラメ hirame

COLUMN

When eating sushi, it's better to start off with light-tasting items such as *tai* and *hirame*, and then move on to richer-tasting *toro* and *uni*. Eating with your hands is OK. To keep sushi from crumbling, dip the topping side into the soy sauce; or if this is difficult, use the ginger as a dipping brush.

寿司を食べる順番は、鯛や平目など味の薄いものから、トロやウニなど味の濃いものへというのがおすすめ。手で食べてもOK。ご飯が崩れないよう、醤油はネタ側につける。つけにくければガリをハケ代わりにしてつけても。

★ The counter for sushi is "*kan*," and each dish usually has 2 kan. Some say that 2 pieces of sushi make 1 kan. 一般に寿司1つで「1貫」と数え、通常2貫ひと皿で供される。寿司2つで1貫とする説もある

"battleship" roll
バトゥシップ ローゥ
軍艦巻き
gunkammaki

cucumber roll
キューカンバァ ローゥ
カッパ巻き
kappamaki

green onion and toro roll
グリーン アニアン アンド トロ ローゥ
ネギトロまき
negitoromaki

wet hand towel — ウェット ハンド タウェゥ — おしぼり — oshibori

conveyor belt — カンヴェイアァ ベゥト — コンベア — kombea

tea tap — ティー タップ — お湯注ぎ口 — oyu sosogiguchi

disposable chopsticks — ディスポウザブゥ チャプスティクス — わりばし — waribashi

teacup — ティー カップ — 湯のみ — yunomi

tea bag — ティー バッグ — お茶パック — ocha pakku

pickled ginger — ピクゥド ジンジャァ — ガリ — gari

soy sauce — ソイ ソース — しょうゆ — shooyu

touch panel — タッチ パネゥ — タッチパネル — tacchi paneru

① After taking your seat, wipe your hands with the hand towel. When a sushi you like comes by, take it. Non-tea drinks need to be ordered.

② Most places have tea bags and teacups on the counter, with taps that dispense hot water.

③ "Gari" —slices of ginger pickled in sweetened vinegar— are also on the counter. Help yourself to some in between dishes, to refresh your mouth.

④ Stack up your used dishes. White dishes are usually cheaper than dishes with designs on them.

⑤ Only certain types of sushi go around on the conveyor, so if you want something different, order it. Some places have intercoms or touch panels for ordering.

⑥ Conveyor belt sushi bars have both traditional kinds of sushi and unusual Western-style toppings, which are also popular. Many also offer soups, salads, and desserts.

⑦ Say "Check, please" to the waiter, and he/she will count your dishes to tally your bill. Some places have devices that automatically count dishes and calculate bills.

① 席に着いたらおしぼりで手を拭き、好みの寿司が回ってきたら自分で取って食べる。お茶以外の飲み物が欲しいときは注文する

② お茶は通常カウンターにあるお茶パックと湯飲みを使って入れる。お湯の出るレバーが設置してあることが多い

③ 薄切りのショウガを甘酢に漬けた「ガリ」もカウンターに置いてある。口をさっぱりさせてくれるので、違う寿司ネタに移る前につまむ

④ 食べ終わった皿は重ねておく。普通、白い皿は値段が安く、絵柄の皿の値段が高い

⑤ コンベアで廻っているネタは限られているので、別のネタが欲しいときには注文しよう。インターホンや液晶タッチパネルで注文できる店もある

⑥ 回転寿司では、伝統的な寿司ネタだけでなく、洋風の変わりネタが人気となっている。また、寿司だけでなく、汁物やサラダ、デザートなどのメニューを用意している店も多い

⑦ 店員に「お勘定をお願いします」と声をかけると皿の枚数を数えて精算してくれる。皿を自動で数えて精算できる機械のある店も

★ There are sushi bars with devices that automatically bring your order to you.
注文した寿司が、目の前に自動的に運ばれる機械を設置した回転寿司店もある

Eating inexpensively

イーティング
イネクスペンスィヴリィ

お金をかけずに食べよう

Okane o kakezu ni tabeyoo

Wanna stop by the ○○ stall?
ワナ スタップ バイ ザ ○○ ストーゥ↑

○○の屋台に寄っていかない？
○○ no yatai ni yotte ikanai?

> **COLUMN**
>
> "*Yatai*" are roofed stalls situated at roadside and other outdoor locations, and are a common sight at festivals and downtown areas at night. Mobile yatai selling boxed lunches in business districts have also become popular recently.
>
> 路傍などの屋外に構えた、屋根のある簡単な店舗が「屋台」。お祭りや夜の繁華街によく見られる。最近では、都市部のオフィス街で弁当を中心としたランチを移動販売する屋台も人気となっている。

はじめよう / 歩こう / 買おう / **食べよう** / 暮らそう / 伝えよう / 知っておこう

Chinese-style noodles in soup seasoned with salt, soy sauce, or miso. The stock is taken from pork, chicken, or fish. Tastes vary by region and restaurant.

麺は中華風で、スープは塩・醤油・味噌味など。だしはトンコツや鶏ガラ、魚介類からとる。店・地域ごとに味の違いが。

ramen
ラーメン
ラーメン
raamen

At *teppan-yaki* stalls, you can enjoy ramen, pot stickers, pig entrails and a variety of other ingredients roasted on a hot iron plate.

鉄板焼の屋台では、焼きラーメンや餃子、ホルモン焼、その他さまざまな具材を使った、大衆的なメニューが気軽に楽しめる。

teppan-yaki
テパンヤキ
鉄板焼
teppan-yaki

Daikon, eggs, konnyaku, fish cake, and other ingredients are simmered in a Japanese-style broth. Flavoring and ingredients vary by region.

和風のだし汁で、大根や卵、コンニャク、ちくわなどの練りものなどを煮込んだもの。味付けや具材は地方によって異なる。

oden
オデン
おでん
oden

Skewered meat and vegetables are coated in a bread crumb batter and deep fried. If the sauce is shared with other customers, don't dip your skewer in the sauce twice.

肉や野菜を串に刺し、パン粉を付けて揚げたもの。ほかの客とソースを共有する店では「ソースの2度づけ禁止」だ。

deep-fried kebab
ディープフライド ケバブ
串カツ
kushikatsu

Fried golf ball-shaped dumplings made from octopus bits dipped into a batter of flour and broth. Osaka has many *takoyaki* shops.

小麦粉とだし汁などで作った生地にタコの小片を入れてゴルフボール大に焼きあげたもの。大阪にはタコ焼店がたくさんある。

takoyaki
タコヤキ
タコ焼
takoyaki

Beef or pork offal is simmered together with vegetables such as cabbage and Chinese chives. The soup is either soy sauce or miso flavored.

下処理した牛や豚のもつ（内臓）をキャベツやニラなどとともにスープで煮込んだ料理。醤油味、味噌味がある。

stewed giblets
ステュード ジブレッツ
もつ鍋
motsunabe

★Fukuoka City's Nakasu, Nagahama, and Tenjin districts are famous for their large concentration of food stalls, known as "*yatai-gai*." 福岡市の中洲、長浜、天神地区は、多くの屋台が集まった「屋台街」で有名

Mainly serving soba and/or udon, they are often found inside and near train stations. A variety of toppings are available. An inexpensive and quick place to eat.

主に日本そば、うどんを出す店で、駅構内や駅前に多い。多様なトッピングがあり、安価で短時間に食べられる。

stand-up soba restaurant
スタンダップ ソバ レストラン

立ち食いそば屋
tachigui sobaya

Thin slices of salty-sweet flavored beef are placed with onions on a bowl of rice. A typical Japanese fast food dish, eaten with pickled ginger and/or raw egg.

甘辛く煮た薄切りの牛肉と玉ネギをご飯に載せたもの。日本の代表的ファーストフード。紅ショウガや生卵を添える。

beef bowl restaurant
ビーフ ボウゥ レストラン

牛丼屋
gyuudon-ya

Restaurants serving rice, soup, and home-style dishes as a set. Inexpensive and—since it includes a vegetable side dish—relatively healthy.

ご飯物、汁物、家庭的なおかず数品がセットになったのが「定食」。割安で、副菜に野菜が入るヘルシーな食事ができる。

set-menu restaurant
セットメニュー レストラン

定食屋
teishokuya

stand-up bar
スタンダップ バーァ

立ち飲み屋
tachinomiya

Counter-only bars often found near stations and under train tracks. Some are connected to liquor shops. Some cheap bars offer all food and drink for 300 yen.

駅前やガード下に多い、カウンターのみの店。酒屋に併設された店や、酒も料理も全品300円といった格安の店も。

fast food restaurant
ファスト フード レストラン

ファーストフード店
faasutofuudoten

International fast food chains also have items on their menu that are unique to Japan. In Japan, people say "*faasuto*" (not "*fasuto*") food.

世界展開のファーストフード店には日本独自のメニューも。「ファストフード」でなく「ファーストフード」と言うのが日本流。

curry restaurant
カリィ レストラン

カレーショップ
karee shoppu

Curry shop chains allow you to choose the level of spiciness and offer a wide variety of curry dishes at a reasonable price. Some even offer home delivery.

辛さが選べ、豊富なメニューを手ごろな値段で楽しめる、チェーン展開のカレーショップがある。宅配サービスのある店も。

department store basement floor
ディパァトメント ストーァ ベイスメント フローァ

デパ地下
depachika

The basement floor food section of department stores, called "*depachika*," is popular for its wide selection of dishes, sweets, and alcohol, and has many upscale items.

デパートの地下食品売場のこと。多様な惣菜、スイーツ、酒類が揃う。生鮮食品もあるが、高級品が多い。

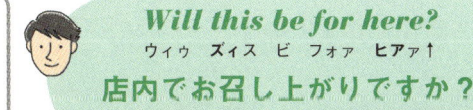

Will this be for here?
ウィゥ ズィス ビ フォァ ヒアァ↑

店内でお召し上がりですか？
Tennai de omeshiagari desu ka?

For here.
フォァ ヒアァ

店内で食べます
Tennai de tabemasu.

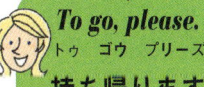

To go, please.
トゥ ゴウ プリーズ

持ち帰ります
Mochikaerimasu.

Going drinking

ゴウイング
ドリンキング
飲みに行こう
Nomi ni ikoo

Wanna go out for a drink tonight?
ワナ ゴウ アウト フォァ ア ドリンク トゥナイト↑

今晩一杯付き合わない？
Komban ippai tsukiawanai?

pub
パブ
居酒屋
izakaya

A pub that serves not only alcohol but a wide range of food dishes. Chains allow you to party with a large group at a low price. They are also a convenient place for families.

酒類とともに多様な料理を出す飲み屋。チェーン店は安く、大勢で騒いでもOK。家族連れも気軽に利用。

A glass of ○○, please.
ア グラス オヴ ○○ プリーズ

○○をグラスでお願いします
○○ o gurasu de onegaishimasu.

sake
サケ
日本酒
nihonshu

Sake is brewed from rice, water, and a mold. Types—such as "*Junmai daiginjō*," and "*Honjōzo*"—vary according to the materials and degree to which the rice is polished.

米と麹、水を主原料とした醸造酒。「純米大吟醸」「本醸造」など、原料と精米の度合いの違いで区別される。

Let's start off with a beer!
レッツ スタート オフ ウィズ ア ビーァ

とりあえずビール！
Toriaezu biiru!

hors d'oeuvre
オーァ ダーヴ
お通し
otooshi

"*Otōshi*" (in Kansai, "*tsukidashi*") is the small, unordered dish that is brought to you together with your drink. Some restaurants charge customers for it.

飲み物と同時に注文しなくても出される小皿料理が「お通し」(関西では「突き出し」とも)。有料の店もある。

shochu
ショーチュー
焼酎
shoochuu

Distilled spirit made from rice, barley, or potatoes. Potato *shōchu* has a strong taste; barley *shōchu*, brown sugar *shōchu*, and Okinawa's *Awamori* are easier to drink.

米や麦、芋などを主原料とした蒸留酒。濃厚な味の芋焼酎、癖の少ない麦焼酎や黒糖焼酎、沖縄の泡盛など。

WORDBANK — Alcohol アルコール

English	Katakana	Japanese	Romaji
draft beer	ドラフト ビーァ	生ビール	namabiiru
low-malt beer	ロウモゥト ビーァ	発泡酒	happooshu
red wine	レッド ワイン	赤ワイン	akawain
white wine	ワイト ワイン	白ワイン	shirowain
plum wine	プラム ワイン	梅酒	umeshu
~ with water	~ ウィズ ウォータァ	~を水割りで	~ o mizuwari de
~ on the rocks	~ オン ザ ロックス	~をロックで	~ o rokku de
cold sake	コウゥド サケ	冷酒	reishu
hot sake	ハット サケ	熱燗	atsukan

distilled liquor with soda
ディスティゥド リカァ ウィズ ソウダ
チューハイ
chuuhai

★Some *izakaya* have an early-evening "happy hour" when alcoholic drinks are served at a discount price.
夕方早い時間のアルコール類の割引、「ハッピーアワー」を実施する居酒屋もある

Food menu

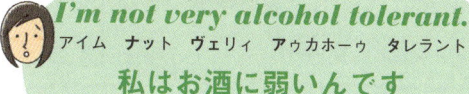

white radish salad
ワイト ラディッシュ サラッド
大根サラダ
daikon sarada

cold tofu
コウゥド トウフ
冷奴
hiyayakko

soy beans
ソイ ビーンズ
枝豆
edamake

deep-fried chicken
ディープフライド チキン
からあげ
karaage

French fries
フレンチ フライズ
フライドポテト
huraido poteto

rice ball
ライス ボーゥ
おにぎり
onigiri

raw fish assortment
ロー フィッシュ アソァートメント
刺身盛り合わせ
sashimi moriawase

Japanese pickles
ジャパニーズ ピクゥズ
漬物
tsukemono

sausage
ソースィッジ
ソーセージ
sooseeji

pizza
ピッツァ
ピザ
piza

fried udon
フライド ウドン
焼きうどん
yakiudon

rice and tea
ライス アンド ティー
お茶漬
ochazuke

I'm not very alcohol tolerant.
アイム ナット ヴェリィ アゥカホーゥ タレラント
私はお酒に弱いんです
Watashi wa osake ni yowaindesu.

I feel sick.
アイ フィーゥ スィック
気持ち悪くなってきたなあ
Kimochi waruku natte kitanaa.

Let's hit another bar!
レッツ ヒット アナザァ バーァ
もう1軒行こうよ！
Moo ikken ikooyo!

---

drinking in one gulp
ドリンキング イン ワン ガゥプ
一気飲み
ikkinomi

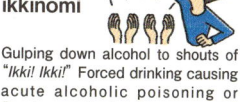

Gulping down alcohol to shouts of "*Ikki! Ikki!*" Forced drinking causing acute alcoholic poisoning or "*aruhara* (alcohol harassment)," has become a social problem.

「イッキ、イッキ」と囃され酒類を一気に飲み干すこと。飲酒の強要が「アルハラ」として問題になっている。

a drunk
ア ドランク
酔っ払い
yopparai

When is the last train?
ウェン イズ ザ ラスト トレイン
終電は何時ですか？
Shuuden wa nanji desu ka?

throw up
スロウ アップ
吐く
haku

hangover
ハンゴウヴァァ
二日酔い
futsukayoi

★Some areas have "shared taxis" that carry multiple passengers on fixed routes late at night when buses and trains are not running. バスや鉄道がない深夜、決まったルートで少人数を運ぶ「乗合タクシー」がある地域も

Getting Along
暮らそう

2-generation household　2世帯住宅

2-generation households are common in Japan.
日本でよく見られる2世帯住宅

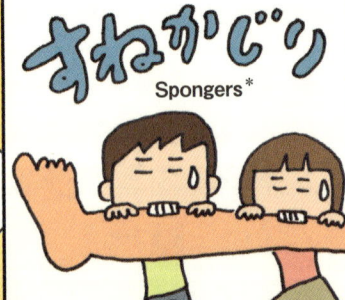

But there's a reason for this...
でもそれは…

住宅ローン且かけて
Help me pay the mortgage!

光熱費も！
And the utility bill!

子育ても手伝って！
And help look after the kids!

まぁまぁ…
Well...

すねかじり
Spongers*

It's not our fault Japanese homes are so expensive!
だって、日本の家、値段が高すぎるんだもん！

*In Japanese, "sponging" off one's parents is called "sunekajiri," or "shin biting."
「すねかじり」＝親などだから生活費や学費をもらっていること。その人のこと。

The sun お日さま

Japanese people like to dry laundry and futons in the sun.
日本人は、洗濯物や布団を太陽の下で乾かすのが好き。

まな板 chopping board
クッション cushion

They also use the sun for sterilizing.
消毒も太陽でするし

ご来光〜！
O holy sun!

On New Year's, people climb mountains to watch the sunrise.
特に元旦は、日の出を見るために山登りする。

お日さまの匂いのする布団！
たまらないわ！く〜！

Ah, nothing beats a futon that smells of the sun!
Yes!

昼間から寝てるけど
あんたの大好きな
お日さままだ出てるよ

While you're there sleeping, the sun you love so much is still out.

67

Housing

ハウズィング

家を借りよう
Ie o kariyoo

I'd like to rent a ~.
アイド ライク トゥ レント ア ～

○○を借りたいのですが
○○ o karitai no desu ga.

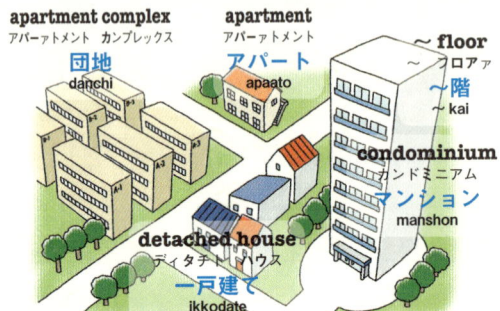

apartment complex アパートメント カンプレックス
団地 danchi

apartment アパートメント
アパート apaato

~ floor ～ フロアァ
～階 ~ kai

condominium カンドミニアム
マンション manshon

detached house ディタチド ハウス
一戸建て ikkodate

~ years old ～ イヤァズ オウゥド
築～年 chiku ~ nen

I'd prefer a bigger room.
アイド プリファーァ ア ビガーァ ルーム

もっと広い部屋がいいのですが
Motto hiroi heya ga ii no desu ga.

near the station ニアァ ザ ステイション
駅から近い eki kara chikai

cheaper	sunny	south-facing	with a nice view
チーパァ	サニィ	サウスフェイスィング	ウィズ ア ナイス ヴュー
もっと安い	日当たりのいい	南向きの	眺めのいい
motto yasui	hiatari no ii	minami muki no	nagame no ii

WORDBANK — Housing 住宅

- **Japanese room** ジャパニーズ ルーム 和室 washitsu
- **bath** バス 浴室 yokushitsu
- **prefabricated bath** プリファブリケイティド バス ユニットバス yunitto basu
- **separate bath and toilet** セパレット バス アンド トイレット バストイレ別 basu toire betsu
- **automatic lock** オートマティック ロック オートロック ootorokku
- **storage room** ストーリッジ ルーム トランクルーム toranku ruumu
- **parking space** パーキング スペイス 駐車場 chuushajoo
- **bicycle parking** バイスィクゥ パーキング 駐輪場 chuurinjoo

COLUMN

"*Shikikin*" is left with the landlord as collateral against failure to pay or damage to property. If at the end of the contract there are no overdue payments and no major damage, the entire amount is returned. "*Reikin*" (usu. 1-2 months' rent) is paid to the landlord as a courtesy.

借り手が家賃滞納や部屋に損害を与えた場合の担保として家主に預けるのが「敷金」。契約終了時、滞納や大きな損害がなければ全額返還されるのが原則となっている。借り手からお礼として家主に払うのが「礼金」。相場は家賃1～2カ月分。

★*Apaato* is used for low-rise wooden and light-gauge steel frame dwellings, and *manshon* for reinforced concrete structures. 木造や軽量鉄骨造の低層住宅が「アパート」、鉄筋コンクリート造の住宅が「マンション」

How large a place do you want?
ハウ ラーァジ ア プレイス ドゥ ユ ワント

どのくらいの広さをご希望ですか？
Donokurai no hirosa o gokiboo desu ka?

Two bedrooms would be nice.
トゥー ベドルームズ ウド ビ ナイス

2LDKがいいのですが
Ni erudiikee ga ii no desu ga.

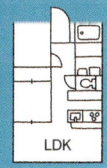

~ tatami mats
タタミ マッツ

~ 畳
~ joo

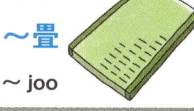

One "jō" (tatami mat) is approx. 1.7 m² (the size varies slightly by area). "Jō" is used not only for tatami rooms but as a general unit of room size measurement.

1畳（畳1枚分）で約1.7㎡（京間、江戸間など地域差がある）。畳敷きの和室でなくても、部屋の大きさを表すのに一般的に使われている単位。

COLUMN

"LDK" is short for "living room, dining room and kitchen." If the "dining room/kitchen" area is more than 8-10 tatami mats in size, it is referred to as "LDK"; otherwise it is called "DK". "2LDK" means "2 rooms + dining room/kitchen."

LDKとは、リビング・ダイニング・キッチンの略。キッチン付きダイニングが大体8〜10畳以上だとLDK、それ未満だとDK。2LDKは居室2つにキッチン付きダイニング1つということ。

brokerage fee
ブロウカリッジ フィー

不動産手数料
fudoosan tesuuryoo

How much is the rent?
ハウ マッチ イズ ザ レント

家賃はいくらですか？
Yachin wa ikura desu ka?

deposit
ディパズィット

敷金
shikikin

key money
キー マニィ

礼金
reikin

management fee
マニジメント フィー

管理費
kanrihi

cancellation
キャンセレイション

解約
kaiyaku

COLUMN

The guarantor in a lease agreement is billed directly when, for example, the rent is not paid. The guarantor cannot refuse to pay. For the lease agreement, a guarantor's seal certification is required, and the seal must go on the contract. People with no guarantor can request one—at a cost—through an agency.

賃貸契約での保証人は、家賃の滞納などの場合に直接請求される連帯保証人。支払いを拒めない。契約時には保証人の印鑑証明、賃借契約書への捺印が必要。保証人がいない場合、保証人代行会社に依頼することも可能。

guarantor certification
ギャランターァ サーァティフィケイション

保証人証明書
hoshoonin shoomeisho

seal certification
スィーゥ サーァティフィケイション

印鑑証明
inkan shoomei

contract renewal fee
カントラクト リニューアゥ フィー

契約更新料
keiyaku kooshinryoo

Lease agreements are generally for 2 years. In many cases, you must pay 1-2 months' rent as a "renewal fee" to renew your contract.

一般に、賃貸住もの契約は2年。契約を更新する際には「契約更新料」として家賃の1〜2カ月分を支払わなければならないことが多い。

★A seal is required for applications, receipts, and other documents; but in many cases, a signature is also acceptable. 日本ではあらゆる申込書や受領書などで印鑑を使用するが、サインで代用される場合も多い

Moving

ムーヴィング
引っ越し
Hikkoshi

Please give me a quote on your moving cost.
プリーズ ギヴ ミ ア クウォウト オン ユアァ ムーヴィング コスト

引っ越しの見積もりをお願いします
Hikkoshi no mitsumori o onegai shimasu.

moving company
ムーヴィング カンパニィ

引っ越し業者

hikkoshi gyoosha

What day do you prefer?
ワット デイ ドゥ ユ プリファァ

ご希望のお日にちはいつですか？
Gokiboo no ohinichi wa itsu desu ka?

I will pack my things myself.
アイ ウィゥ パック マイ スィングズ マイセゥフ

荷造りは自分でやります
Nizukuri wa jibun de yarimasu.

🌸 COLUMN

You should decide on a moving company by at least 3 weeks prior to your desired moving date. First, try getting quotes from different movers by phone or the Internet. Many moving companies provide boxes and other packing materials free of charge.

引っ越しが決まったら、遅くとも希望日の3週間前までには引っ越し業者を決めたい。まずはインターネットや電話で業者に見積もりをお願いしよう。荷造りに必要なダンボールなどの梱包材は無料で提供してくれる引っ越し業者が多い。

● **Packing materials**　梱包材

dolly
ダリィ
台車
daisha

cardboard box
カーァドボーァド バクス
ダンボール
dambooru

hanger box
ハンガァ バクス
ハンガーボックス
hangaa bokkusu

futon bag
フトン バッグ
布団袋
huton bukuro

futon compression bag
フトン カンプレション バッグ
布団圧縮袋
futon asshuku bukuro

packing tape
パキング テイプ
ガムテープ
gamuteepu

cushioning material
クショニング マテリアゥ
気泡緩衝材
kihoo kanshoozai

★Cushioning material is commonly referred to by brand names such as Air Caps, Air Cushion, and Puchi Puchi. 気泡緩衝材は、一般にエアキャップやエアクッション、プチプチなどの商標で呼ばれている

Please handle this with care.
プリーズ ハンドゥ ズィス ウィズ ケアァ

気をつけて運んでください
Ki o tsukete hakonde kudasai.

Please put the ○○ here.
プリーズ プット ザ ○○ ヒアァ

○○はここに置いてください
○○ wa koko ni oite kudasai.

unpacking
アンパキング

荷解き
nihodoki

cast-off items
キャストオフ アイテムズ

不用品
fuyoohin

My name is ○○. I just moved in (next door).
マイ ネイム イズ ○○ アイ ジャスト ムーヴド イン (ネクスト ドアァ)

新しく引っ越してきた○○です。よろしくお願いします
Atarashiku hikkoshitekita ○○ desu. Yoroshiku onegai shimasu.

landlord
ランドロアド

大家さん
ooya san

housewarming gift
ハウスウォーミング ギフト

引っ越し祝い
hikkoshi iwai

When a friend buys a home, a present worth 5,000-10,000 yen, or a cash gift, is commonly given. Housewarming gifts are not needed for moves to a rented place.

友人が住宅を購入したら、5千円〜1万円くらいのプレゼントかお金をあげる。賃貸への引っ越しなら必要ない。

● Greeting new neighbors   引っ越してきたときのあいさつ

house
家

condominium / apartment
マンション・アパート

next door and across the street
向こう三軒両隣

next door, above and below
両隣・上下階

After moving, pay a courtesy visit to your new neighbors, and bring a gift. Call on your immediate neighbors— those next door and across the street if you live in a detached house, and those next-door, above, and below you if you live in a condominium. A gift of towels or sweets, worth around 500 yen, is sufficient. Try to visit on the day of your move. Information about family composition, pets, etc. should also be conveyed. If you live in a rented home in an urban area with many single-person households, however, courtesy calls may be unnecessary as many people find such socializing troublesome.

引っ越してきたときは、近所に手みやげを持ってあいさつに行く。一戸建ての場合は「向こう三軒両隣」、マンションの場合は両隣と上下階の人にあいさつに回る。手みやげはタオルやお菓子で、金額は500円程度が無難。なるべく引っ越し当日に行こう。家族構成やペットの有無なども伝えておきたい。ただし、都会のひとり暮らしの多い賃貸住宅では近所づきあいをわずらわしく思う人も多いので、引っ越しのあいさつはしなくてもいい。

🌸 COLUMN

Moving procedures
Before moving, you must submit "change of address" notices to the following:
* Your local government office
* The post office (to have your mail forwarded)
* Electric/gas/water/phone companies, banks, credit card companies, etc.

After moving, don't forget to submit a "moving-in" notice to your government office.

引っ越しのときの手続き
引っ越し前には、次のような手続きが必要となる。
* 役所で転出届を出す
* 郵便局に転居届を出す（郵便物を転送してもらえる）
* 電気・ガス・水道・電話、銀行やクレジットカードなどの住所変更手続きをする

引っ越し後には役所で転入届を出すのを忘れずに。

★See p. 78 for details on socializing with neighbors.
近所づきあいについてはP.78参照

Visiting a home

ヴィズィティング ア ホウム
家を訪問しよう
Ie o hoomon shiyoo

Please come in.
プリーズ カム イン
どうぞおあがりください
Doozo oagari kudasai.

slippers スリパァズ スリッパ surippa

shoe box シューバクス 靴箱 kutsubako

visiting gift ヴィズィティング ギフト 手みやげ temiyage

entrance エントランス 玄関 genkan

Sorry to disturb you.
サリィ トゥ ディスターァブ ユ
おじゃまします
Ojamashimasu.

COLUMN

Etiquette when visiting a home
As a rule, bring a gift (sweets, alcohol, etc.) when visiting someone's home. You're supposed to say "*Tsumaranai mono desu ga*, ('This is a boring gift')" when presenting a gift, but nowadays, saying "This cake is from a well-known shop" is also acceptable. When paying a formal visit, take off your coat before entering. After taking off your shoes, line them up against the edge, toes facing out.

家を訪問するときのマナー
頻繁に行き来している相手でなければ、訪問の際には手みやげを持っていこう。お菓子やお酒などが一般的。贈り物を渡すとき日本人は「つまらないものですが」と言うとされているが、最近では変わってきている。「評判のいいお店のケーキなんですよ」などと言って渡すと好印象になるだろう。家に入るときは、改まった訪問ならコート類は玄関に入る前に脱いでおく。靴は脱いだら向きを直し、端に寄せる。

stairs ステアァズ 階段 kaidan

elevator エレヴェイタァ エレベーター erebeetaa

hall ホーゥ 廊下 rooka

flooring フローリング フローリング furooringu

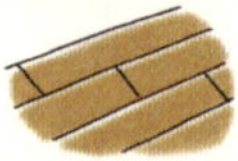

bath heater and dryer バス ヒータァ アンド ドライヤァ 浴室暖房乾燥機 yokushitsu danboo kansooki

living room リヴィング ルーム リビングルーム ribingu ruumu

bedroom ベドルーム 寝室 shinshitsu

Baths equipped not only with ventilation and heating but also a laundry-drying function are convenient. Nearly all new condominiums have this feature.

換気や冬場の暖房だけでなく、浴室を洗濯乾燥室として使えて便利。最近の新築マンションにはほぼ付いている。

★"Flooring" is Japlish. In English, "flooring" is a broader term for all floors, and is not limited to "floorboards."
フローリングは和製英語。英語のflooringは木の床張りに限らず「床、床張り」の意味

●Traditional Japanese house 伝統的な日本の家

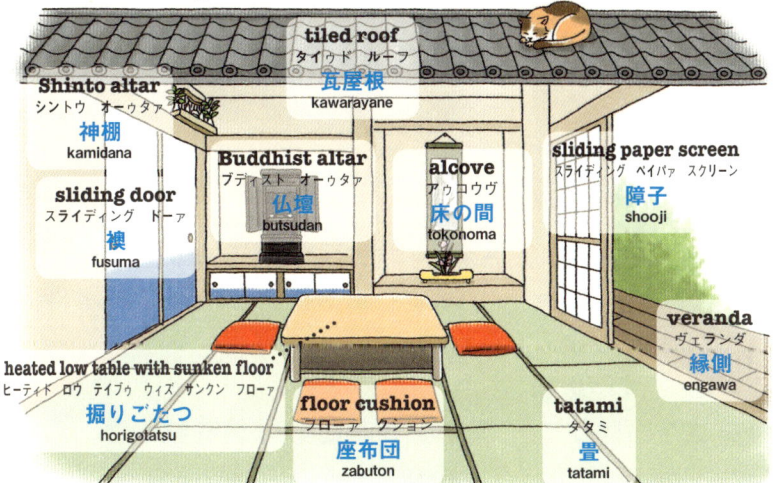

- **tiled roof** タイゥド ルーフ 瓦屋根 kawarayane
- **Shinto altar** シントウ オーゥタァ 神棚 kamidana
- **Buddhist altar** ブディスト オーゥタァ 仏壇 butsudan
- **sliding door** スライディング ドーァ 襖 fusuma
- **alcove** アゥコウヴ 床の間 tokonoma
- **sliding paper screen** スライディング ペイパァ スクリーン 障子 shooji
- **veranda** ヴェランダ 縁側 engawa
- **heated low table with sunken floor** ヒーティド ロウ テイブゥ ウィズ サンクン フローァ 掘りごたつ horigotatsu
- **floor cushion** フローァ クションン 座布団 zabuton
- **tatami** タタミ 畳 tatami

May I use your restroom?
メイ アイ ユーズ ユアァ レストルーム↑
お手洗いを借りていいですか？
Otearai o karite ii desu ka?

It's down the hall on the left.
イッツ ダウン ザ ホーゥ オン ザ レフト
廊下に出て左ですよ
Rooka ni dete hidari desu yo.

🌸 COLUMN

Japanese toilets
In Japan, bidet toilets have become standard. Newer toilets may also be equipped with automatic lid/flushing and/or deodorizer functions. Many homes have separate restroom slippers, so be careful not to step out in the wrong slippers.

日本のトイレ
日本では温水洗浄便座が一般家庭に普及している。最近では、ふたの自動開閉や便器洗浄、消臭機能なども搭載されている。また家庭ではトイレで専用のスリッパを履くことが多い。トイレから出るとき履いて出てこないように。

- **kitchen** キチン 台所 daidokoro
- **bath** バス お風呂 ofuro

I should get going.
アイ シュド ゲット ゴウイング
そろそろ失礼します
Sorosoro shitsurei shimasu.

Thank you for coming.
サンキュ フォア カミング
今日は来てくれてありがとう
Kyoo wa kitekurete arigatoo.

★In formal situations, sit on your knees. If your host says, "Please make yourself comfortable," you can change position. 改まった場では正座する。「お楽にしてください」と言われたら正座を崩してもいい

Housework

ハウスワーク
家事
Kaji

Could you clean this room?
クジュ クリーン ズィス ルーム↑
部屋を掃除してくれない？
Heya o soojishite kurenai?

cleaned up
クリーンド アップ
きれいに片付いた
kireini katazuita

messy
メスィイ
ちらかった
chirakatta

vacuum
ヴァキューム
掃除機をかける
soojiki o kakeru

wipe the table
ワイプ ザ テイブゥ
テーブルを拭く
teeburu o fuku

wipe the window
ワイプ ザ ウィンドウ
窓を拭く
mado o fuku

take out the garbage
テイク アウト ザ ガーァビッジ
ごみを出す
gomi o dasu

wax the floor
ワックス ザ フローァ
床にワックスをかける
yuka ni wakkusu o kakeru

WORDBANK — Cleaning 掃除

broom	ブルーム	ほうき	hooki
dustpan	ダストパン	ちりとり	chiritori
duster	ダスタァ	はたき	hataki
trash can	トラッシュ キャン	ごみ箱	gomi bako
trash bag	トラッシュ バッグ	ごみ袋	gomi bukuro
cleaning rag	クリーニング ラグ	ぞうきん	zookin
sweep	スウィープ	掃く	haku
rinse	リンス	すすぐ	susugu
polish	パリッシュ	磨く	migaku

I'll wash the dishes.
アイゥ ワシュ ザ ディシィズ
私がお皿を洗うわ
Watashi ga osara o arau wa.

Then I'll wipe the dishes.
ゼン アイゥ ワイプ ザ ディシィズ
じゃあ僕がお皿を拭こう
Jaa boku ga osara o fukoo.

sponge スパンジ スポンジ suponji
dishcloth ディッシュクロス ふきん fukin
cleaner クリーナァ 洗剤 senzai
drain basket ドレイン バスケット 水切りかご mizukirikago

★When washing dishes, many people in the West do not rinse off the detergent much before drying; but Japanese people rinse off dishes thoroughly. 欧米では皿を洗う際、洗剤をあまり流さずふきんで拭く人が多い

do the laundry
ドゥ ザ ランドリィ

洗濯する

sentaku suru

hang the laundry
ハング ザ ランドリィ

洗濯物を干す

sentakumono o hosu

take in the laundry
テイク イン ザ ランドリィ

洗濯物を取り込む

sentakumono o torikomu

WORDBANK — Laundry 洗濯

laundry detergent	ランドリィ ディターァジェント	洗濯洗剤	sentaku senzai
bleach	ブリーチ	漂白剤	hyoohakuzai
fabric softener	ファブリック ソフナァ	柔軟剤	juunanzai
laundry starch	ランドリィ スターチ	洗濯のり	sentakunori
washing machine	ワシング マシーン	洗濯機	sentakki
dryer	ドライヤァ	乾燥機	kansooki
spin-dry	スピンドライ	脱水機にかける	dassuiki ni kakeru
hanger	ハンガァ	ハンガー	hangaa
laundry pole	ランドリィ ボウ	物干し竿	monohoshi zao
clothespin	クロウズピン	洗濯ばさみ	sentaku basami
iron	アイアン	アイロンをかける	airon o kakeru
stain	ステイン	しみ	shimi
wrinkles	リンクゥズ	しわ	shiwa
fold	フォウウド	たたむ	tatamu

I took that suit to the cleaner's.
アイ トゥック ザット スート トゥ ザ クリーナァズ

あのスーツはクリーニングに出しといたよ

Ano suutsu wa kuriiningu ni dashitoita yo.

Can you get it from the cleaner's?
キャン ユ ゲット イット フロム ザ クリーナァズ↑

クリーニング屋に取りに行ってきてくれない？

Kuriininguya ni torini ittekite kurenai?

remove a stain
リムーヴ ア ステイン

しみ抜きする

shiminuki suru

water-repellant treated
ウォータァリペラント トリーティド

撥水加工の

hassuikakoo no

look after a pet
ルック アフタァ ア ペット

ペットの世話する

petto no sewa o suru

feed
フィード

えさをやる

esa o yaru

put a crease in
プット ア クリース イン

折り目をつける

orime o tsukeru

I have to water the plants.
アイ ハフ トゥ ウォータァ ザ プランツ

植木に水をやらなきゃ

Ueki ni mizu o yaranakya.

weed
ウィード

雑草を取る

zassoo o toru

★Many people in Japan hang their laundry outside, but to preserve the cityscape, some condominiums prohibit this practice. 日本では洗濯物を外に干すことが多いが、最近は景観のため禁止するマンションも

Cooking

クキング
料理
Ryoori

How do you make this dish?
ハウ ドゥ ユ メイク ズィス ディッシュ

この料理はどうやって作るの？
Kono ryoori wa dooyatte tsukuru no?

Add ○○ before eating.
アッド ○○ ビフォア イーティング

これは○○をつけて食べてね
Kore wa ○○ o tsukete tabete ne.

boil ボイゥ ゆでる yuderu	**stew** ステュー 煮る niru
stir-fry スターァフライ 炒める itameru	**fry (in oil)** フライ（イン オイゥ） （油で）揚げる (abura de) ageru

WORDBANK — Cooking utensils 調理器具

English	カタカナ	日本語	Romaji
pot	パット	鍋	nabe
lid	リッド	ふた	huta
frying pan	フライング パン	フライパン	furaipan
kitchen knife	キチン ナイフ	包丁	hoochoo
chopping board	チョピング ボード	まな板	manaita
strainer	ストレイナァ	ざる	zaru
ladle	レイドゥ	おたま	otama
rice scoop	ライス スクープ	しゃもじ	shamoji
spatula	スパチュラ	フライ返し	furaigaeshi

●Cutting ingredients　材料の切り方

cut into thin pieces カット イントゥ スィン ピースィズ
薄切りする　usugiri suru

cut into fine strips カット イントゥ ファイン ストリプス
千切りする　sengiri suru

dice ダイス
さいの目切りする　sainomegiri suru

cut into tiny pieces カット イントゥ タイニィ ピースィズ
みじん切りする　mijingiri suru

cut into rectangular strips カット イントゥ レクタングラァ ストリプス
拍子切りする　hyooshigiri suru

chop into large pieces チョップ イントゥ ラーァジ ピースィズ
ぶつ切りする　butsugiri suru

bake in an oven ベイク イン アン アヴン オーブンで焼く oobun de yaku	**grill lightly** グリゥ ライトリィ あぶる aburu
grill on a mesh グリゥ オン ア メッシュ 網焼きする amiyaki suru	**steam** スティーム 蒸す musu
mash マッシュ つぶす tsubusu	**grate** グレイト すりおろす suriorosu

★Japanese homes incorporate a wide variety of dishes from around the world, such as North African tajine.
北アフリカのタジン鍋が流行するなど、日本では家庭でも世界各国の料理を幅広く取り入れる

How does that dish taste?
ハウ ダズ ザット ディッシュ テイスト

その料理の味はどう?
Sono ryoori no aji wa doo?

bad-tasting
バッドテイスティング
まずい
mazui

It's really tasty!
イッツ リアリィ テイスティ
すごくおいしいよ!
Sugoku oishii yo!

salty
ソーゥティ
しょっぱい
shoppai

sweet
スウィート
甘い
amai

It's too spicy!
イッツ トゥー スパイスィ
辛すぎるよ!
Karasugiru yo!

stock
スタック
だし
dashi

In Japanese cooking, stock is commonly extracted from dried kelp, dried shiitake, or bonito flakes by soaking or boiling. It is the basic flavor of Japanese food.

だしは、コンブ、カツオ節、干シイタケ、煮干などの乾物を水に浸したり、煮出したもの。日本料理基本の旨み。

WORDBANK — Taste expressions 味の表現

English	カタカナ	日本語	romaji
sour	サウアァ	すっぱい	suppai
bitter	ビタァ	苦い	nigai
astrigent	アストリンジェント	渋い	shibui
greasy	グリースィ	油っぽい	aburappoi
rich	リッチ	こってりした	kotteri shita
light	ライト	あっさりした	assari shita
crispy	クリスピィ	カリカリした	karikari shita
soggy	ソギィ	しけた	shiketa
thick	スィック	とろみがある	toromi ga aru

sweet cooking wine
スウィート クキング ワイン
みりん
mirin

Glutinous rice is blended with malted rice, aged in distilled liquor, and strained. Adds sweetness, and enhances the flavor of stew.

蒸したもち米を米麹に混ぜ、焼酎やアルコールを加えて熟成させて絞ったもの。料理の甘みづけ、煮物の風味づけなどに使われる。

WORDBANK — Seasoning 調味料

sugar	シュガァ	砂糖	satoo
salt	ソーゥト	塩	shio
soy sauce	ソイ ソース	しょうゆ	chooyu
fermented bean paste	ファァメンティド ビーン ペイスト	みそ	miso
vinegar	ヴィニガァ	酢	su
pepper	ペパァ	こしょう	koshoo
mustard	マスタッド	カラシ	karashi
red pepper	レッド ペパァ	唐辛子	toogarashi
sesame oil	セサミ オイゥ	ごま油	gomaabura

★Flavoring varies by region. For example, the soup in udon is soy sauce-rich and dark in color in *Kanto*, but is lighter in color in *Kansai*. 味付けは地方それぞれ。うどんの汁も、関東は醤油が強く色も濃いが、関西では色が薄い

Socializing with neighbors

ソウシャライズィング ウィズ ネイバァズ
近所づきあい
Kinjo zukiai

separation of garbage
セパレイション オヴ ガーァビッジ
ごみの分別
gomi no bumbetsu

garbage collection point
ガーァビッジ コレクション ポイント
ごみ置き場
gomiokiba

🌸 COLUMN
Garbage duty
Neighborhood households often take turns doing "garbage duty," a troublesome job that not only requires you to keep the local collection point clean but may also entail separating garbage that was not separated properly or returning garbage to its "owner."

ごみ当番
ごみ置き場の掃除を近所で順番に行う「ごみ当番」が決められている場合がある。きちんと分別せずに回収されなかったごみを分別し直したり、誰が出したものか調べて返却に行かなければならなかったりなど苦労も多い。

Today is not a garbage day.
トゥデイ イズ ナット ア ガーァビッジ デイ
今日はごみ出しの日じゃありませんよ
Kyoo wa gomidashi no hi ja arimasen yo.

Sorry, I made a mistake.
サリィ アイ メイド ア ミステイク
すみません。まちがえてしまいました
Sumimasen. Machigaete shimaimashita.

🌸 COLUMN
Greeting neighbors
Try to greet people you see in your neighborhood with a friendly "Good morning" or "Good evening", even if you are not sure who they are. In addition to saying "Hello" when meeting someone on the elevator, say "Excuse me (*Osakini shitsurei shimasu*)" if you get off first, or "Good night" if it is night. Some people prefer to maintain their privacy, so be careful to avoid prying into personal affairs.

近所の人とのあいさつ
近所で会う人には、顔に覚えのない人でも「おはようございます」「こんばんは」などとあいさつをしよう。マンションのエレベーターでほかの住人と乗り合せたら、「こんにちは」などのあいさつはもちろん、先に下りるときには「お先に失礼します」、夜なら「おやすみなさい」などと言おう。プライバシーを守りたい人もいるので、深く立ち入った話をするのは要注意。

---

unburnable garbage
アンバァナブゥ ガーァビッジ
燃えないごみ
moenai gomi

burnable garbage
バーナブゥ ガーァビッジ
燃えるごみ
moeru gomi

oversized garbage
オウヴァサイズド ガーァビッジ
粗大ごみ
sodai gomi

garbage disposal ticket
ガーァビッジ ディスポウザゥ ティケット
ごみ処理券
gomi shoriken

plastic bottles
プラスティック バトゥズ
ペットボトル
pettobotoru

bottles
バトゥズ
びん
bin

cans
キャンズ
缶
kan

recyclable garbage
リサイクラブゥ ガーァビッジ
リサイクルごみ
risaikuru gomi

wastepaper
ウェイストペイパァ
古紙
koshi

cardboard boxes
カーァドボーァド バクスィズ
ダンボール
danbooru

★Oversized garbage is put out after placing a request to the local government and paying a fee.
粗大ごみを出すときは、あらかじめ自治体に申し込み、手数料を払う

neighborhood association
ネイバァフッド アソスィエイション

町内会
choonaikai

Voluntary groups comprised of local residents. Single people often do not bother to join. They conduct evacuation drills and cleaning projects, put on shrine fairs, obon dances, and shrine-carrying festivals in summer; and in winter they host events such as the New Year's rice-cake pounding.

町内会は、住民によって組織されている任意団体。単身者などは加入していない人が多い。多くの町内会では、道路や公園等の清掃、避難訓練のほか、さまざまな行事もする。夏には縁日や盆踊り、神社の氏子を中心にしてお神輿を担ぐ夏祭り、冬には獅子舞やもちつき大会などの正月行事も開催する。

●summer 夏

summer festival
サマァ フェスティヴァゥ
夏祭り
natsumatsuri

portable shrine
ポーァタブル シュライン
お神輿
omikoshi

shrine fair
シュライン フェアァ
縁日
en-nichi

Bon Festival dance
ボン フェスティヴァゥ ダンス
盆踊り
bon-odori

●winter 冬

rice-cake pounding
ライスケイク パウンディング
もちつき大会
mochitsuki taikai

Lion Dance
ライアン ダンス
獅子舞
shishimai

🌸 COLUMN

"Kairanban"
The "*kairanban*" is a file circulated by the neighborhood association that includes association decisions and event notices. After reading it, enter your seal in the space on the front and pass it on to the next home.

回覧板
町内会で回し読みする情報ファイルを「回覧板」と呼ぶ。主に町内会の決定事項やイベントのお知らせなどの伝達を目的としている。通常表紙の下部には印鑑を押す欄が設けてあるので、読み終えたらそこに捺印して、次の家に回す。

I received many apples, so please have some.
アイ リスィーヴド メニィ アプゥズ ソウ プリーズ ハヴ サム
リンゴをたくさんもらったので、少しどうぞ
Ringo o takusan moratta node, sukoshi doozo.

sharing
シェアリング
おすそ分け
osusowake

"*Osusowake*" is the sharing with neighbors of something you have received or made. If a neighbor shares something with you, return the favor with your own "*osusowake*."

何かをたくさんもらったり、作り過ぎたりしたときにご近所に分けてあげるのが「おすそわけ」。何かをいただいたら、同じように「おすそわけ」でお返ししよう。

Could you be a little more quiet at night?
クジュ ビア リトゥ モアァ クワイエット アット ナイト↑
夜はもう少し静かにしてもらえませんか？
Yoru wa moosukoshi shizukani shite moraemasen ka?

I'm very sorry. I will be more careful.
アイム ヴェリィ サリィ アイ ウィゥ ビ モアァ ケアァフゥ
申し訳ありませんでした。今後気をつけます
Mooshiwake arimasen deshita. Kongo ki o tsukemasu.

complain
コンプレイン
苦情を言う
kujoo o iu

noise
ノイズ
騒音
soo-on

★If you receive a complaint about noise, apologize immediately if the complaint is legitimate.
騒音などについて苦情を言われたら、心当たりがある場合はすぐ謝ろう

Weddings and funerals
ウェディング アンド フューネラゥズ

結婚式と葬式
Kekkonshiki to sooshiki

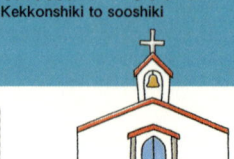

Congratulations on your wedding.
コングラチュレイションズ オン ユアァ ウェディング

ご結婚おめでとうございます
Gokekkon omedetoo gozaimasu.

I wish you the best.
アイ ウィッシュ ユ ザ ベスト

お幸せにね
Oshiawaseni ne.

---

wedding ceremony
ウェディング セレモニィ
結婚式
kekkonshiki

wedding party
ウェディング パァティ
披露宴
hiroo-en

groom
グルーム
新郎
shinroo

cake cutting
ケイク カティング
ケーキ入刀
keeki nyuutoo

bride
ブライド
新婦
shimpu

emcee
エムスィー
司会
shikai

take-away gift
テイカウェイ ギフト
引き出物
hikidemono

congratulatory telegram
コングラチュレイトリィ テレグラム
祝電
shukuden

wedding gift
ウェディング ギフト
結婚祝い
kekkon iwai

Bring monetary gifts to the wedding party, but send presents in advance. For a friend or coworker, 20,000-50,000 yen is appropriate. Use new banknotes, and place them in an envelope.

お金なら披露宴に持参、品物なら事前に送る。友人や同僚なら2〜5万円が相場。お金はご祝儀袋に新札を入れて。

COLUMN
Wedding invitations and gifts
In the West, wedding invitations are generally sent out to couples, but in Japan, it is often only the friend of the bride or groom that is invited. Moreover, there is usually no "bridal registry" from which to select a present for the new couple.

結婚式への招待とお祝い
欧米では結婚式や披露宴にはカップルで招かれるのが普通だが、日本では友人である本人だけのことも多い。また欧米で一般的な「ブライダル・レジストリ（新郎新婦が欲しい物をリストにし、そこから贈り物を選ぶ）」はあまりない。

WORDBANK — Marriage 結婚

English	Katakana	Japanese	Romaji
get engaged	ゲット エンゲイジド	婚約する	kon-yaku suru
engagement ring	エンゲイジメント リング	婚約指輪	kon-yaku yubiwa
wedding ring	ウェディング リング	結婚指輪	kekkon yubiwa
go-between	ゴウビトウィーン	仲人	nakoodo
speech	スピーチ	スピーチ	supiichi
formal wear	フォーァマゥ ウェアァ	礼服	reifuku
change of dress	チェインジ オヴ ドレス	お色直し	oironaoshi
relatives	リラティヴズ	親族	shinzoku
honeymoon	ハニムーン	新婚旅行	shinkon ryokoo

★A variety of weddings are conducted in Japan—Christian, Shinto, Buddhist, secular, etc.—and the style of wedding is often unrelated to the host's religion. 日本では、多様な様式の結婚式がある。宗教とはあまり関係ない

Please accept my condolences.
ブリーズ アクセプト マイ コンドゥレンスィズ
このたびはご愁傷様です
Konotabi wa goshuushoosama desu.

May his (her) soul rest in peace.
メイ ヒズ (ハァ) ソウゥ レスト イン ピース
心よりご冥福をお祈りします
Kokoro yori gomeifuku o oinori shimasu.

wake
ウェイク
お通夜
otsuya

funeral service
フューネラゥ サーァヴィス
お葬式
osooshiki

silent prayer
サイレント プレアァ
黙祷
mokutoo

farewell ceremony
フェアァウェゥ セレモニィ
告別式
kokubetsushiki

chief mourner
チーフ モーァナァ
喪主
moshu

mourning dress
モーァニング ドレス
喪服
mofuku

prayer beads
プレアァ ビーズ
数珠
juzu

condolence
コンドゥレンス
お悔やみ
okuyami

COLUMN
How to offer incense
① Bow to the priest, bereaved, and other mourners, and proceed to the altar. Bow to the image of the deceased. Hang the beads from your left hand.
② Take a pinch of incense with your right hand, raise it to eye level, and drop it on the burner. Do this 1-3 times.
③ Join your palms. Back up slightly, bow to the priest, bereaved, and mourners, and return to your seat.

お焼香のしかた
①僧侶、遺族、列席者の順に一礼してから祭壇の前に進み、遺影に一礼。数珠は左手にかけておく。
②右手で香を少しつまみ、目の高さまで上げてから、香炉に香をくべる。これを1～3回行う。
③遺影に向かい合掌。少し下がって僧侶と遺族、列席者に一礼し席に戻る。

WORDBANK — Funerals お葬式

condolence call	コンドレンス コーゥ	弔問	choomon
words of condolence	ワーズ オヴ コンドレンス	弔辞	chooji
telegram of condolence	テレグラム オヴ コンドレンス	弔電	chooden
joining of palms	ジョイニング オヴ パゥムズ	合掌	gasshoo
carrying out of coffin	キャリイング アウト オヴ コーフィン	出棺	shukkan
cremation	クリメイション	火葬	kasoo
ashes	アシィズ	遺骨	ikotsu
condolence return gift	コンドゥレンス リターァン ギフト	香典返し	kooden gaeshi

funeral offering
フューネラゥ オファリング
お香典
okooden

For a friend or work acquaintance, offer a condolence gift of 5,000-20,000 yen at the wake or farewell ceremony. Put the money in an envelope with "*goreizen*" written in light ink.
友人や仕事関係者の場合、5,000円～2万円を「御霊前」と書かれた香典袋に入れ通夜か告別式で渡す。

★In Japan, people normally wear black mourning dress to funerals, but for the wake, gray is acceptable. Prayer beads are not required. 日本のお葬式では黒の喪服が一般的。お通夜はグレーなどでもOK。数珠はなくてもいい

Pregnancy and childbirth

プレグナンスィ アンド
チャイゥドバース

妊娠と出産
Ninshin to shussan

Are you expecting?
ァァ ユ イクスペクティング↑
ひょっとしておめでた？
Hyottoshite omedeta?

Yes, I'm ~ months' pregnant.
イエス、アイム ～ マンツ プレグナント
ええ。今妊娠～カ月なの
Ee. Ima ninshin ~ kagetsu nano.

How are you feeling?
ハウ ァァ ユ フィーリング
体調はどう？
Taichoo wa doo?

I'm suffering from morning sickness.
アイム サファリング フロム モーニング スィックネス
つわりが大変なの
Tsuwari ga taihen nano.

When is the due date?
ウェン イズ ザ デュー デイト
出産予定日はいつ？
Shussan yoteibi wa itsu?

My feet are swollen.
マイ フィート ァァ スウォルン
足がむくんでるの
Ashi ga mukunderu no.

have leg cramps
ハヴ レッグ クランプス
脚がつる
ashi ga tsuru

have bleeding
ハヴ ブリーディング
出血する
shukketsu suru

have a miscarriage
ハヴ ァ ミスキャリッジ
流産する
ryuuzan suru

COLUMN

Expectant mothers have a custom of putting on a waistband on the first "day of the dog" (see p.114) in their fifth month and praying for a healthy childbirth. This prayer can be done at most shrines, but Suitengu shrines are most famous. Many shrines only conduct purifications for waistbands of bleached cotton cloth.

妊娠5カ月目に入った最初の戌（いぬ）の日（P.114参照）に「腹帯」を締めて母子の健康を祈願する風習がある。この安産祈願は多くの神社でできるが、特に水天宮が有名。お祓いしてもらう腹帯はさらしの布に限る神社が多い。

I have stomach contractions.
アイ ハヴ スタマック コントラクションズ
おなかが張ります
Onaka ga harimasu.

My waters broke.
マイ ウォータァズ ブロウク
破水したようです
Hasui shita yoodesu.

★If you become pregnant, report it to the local government and get a "boshi techō," a booklet for recording pre- and post-partum changes, and the child's growth. 妊娠したら自治体に届け出て「母子手帳」をもらう

My contractions are 10 minutes apart.
マイ コントラクションズ アァ テン ミニッツ アパート

陣痛が10分おきになりました
Jintsuu ga jippun oki ni narimashita.

start contractions
スタート コントラクションズ

陣痛が始まる
jintsuu ga hajimaru

ordinary delivery
オーァディナリィ デリヴァリィ

普通分娩
hutsuu bumben

C-section
スィーセクション

帝王切開
teioo sekkai

painless delivery
ペインレス デリヴァリィ

無痛分娩
mutsuu bumben

COLUMN

Whereas mothers in the West sometimes leave the hospital the day after giving birth, in Japan women usually stay in the hospital 5-7 days after normal delivery, or 10-14 days after C-section. Moreover, it is not unusual for women to stay at the home of their own parents before and after childbirth.

普通分娩の場合、欧米では翌日退院も珍しくないが、日本での入院は普通分娩なら5〜7日程度、帝王切開なら10日〜2週間程度が多い。また、産前産後を妻の実家で過ごす「里帰り出産」をするケースも珍しくない。

WORDBANK — Pregnancy 妊娠

ultrasound	アゥトラサウンド	超音波検査	choo-ompa kensa
gynecological examination	ガイナカラジカゥ イグザミネイション	内診	naishin
fetal movement	フィートゥ ムーヴメント	胎動	taidoo
fetus	フィータス	胎児	taiji
gestational toxicosis	ジェステイショナゥ タクスィコウスィス	妊娠中毒症	ninshin chuudokushoo
breech delivery	ブリーチ デリヴァリィ	逆子	sakago
umbilical cord	アンビリカゥ コーァド	へその緒	heso no o

Congratulations on the birth of your baby.
コングラチュレイションズ オン ザ バース オヴ ユアァ ベイビィ

出産おめでとう
Shussan omedetoo.

Thank you. Everything went fine.
サンキュ エヴリスィング ウェント ファイン

ありがとう。安産だったのよ
Arigatoo. Anzan dattano yo.

Baby gift
ベイビィ ギフト

出産祝い
shussan iwai

Slightly oversized baby clothing worth 5,000-10,000 yen is a safe choice. If you are the recipient, send a return gift worth half the price of the item received.

少し大きめのベビー服が無難。金額は5,000円〜1万円。お祝いをもらったら半額程度で内祝を送る。

It was a difficult delivery.
イット ワズ ア ディフィカゥト デリヴァリィ

難産でした
Nanzan deshita.

★More men in Japan are choosing to be present at childbirth, but some hospitals still do not allow this practice.
日本でも夫の立会い出産が増えてきたが、立会いを受け付けない産院もある

Parenting

ペアレンティング

育児・子供と遊ぶ
Ikuji, kodomo to asobu

Can you change the baby's diapers?
キャン ユ チェインジ ザ ベイビィズ ダイパァ↑

赤ちゃんのオムツを替えてくれる？
Akachan no omutsu o kaete kureru?

give formula
ギヴ フォーァミュラ
ミルクをあげる
miruku o ageru

breastfeed
ブレストフィード
母乳をあげる
bonyuu o ageru

Can I hold him (her)?
キャナイ ホウゥド ヒム (ハァ)↑

抱っこしてもいいかしら？
Dakko shitemo ii kashira?

Sure. He (She) can hold his(her) head up now.
シュアァ ヒー (シー) キャン ホウゥド ヒズ (ハァ) ヘッド アップ ナウ

ええ。首も据わってきたのよ
Ee. Kubi mo suwatte kitano yo.

roll over
ローゥ オウヴァ
寝返りする
negaeri suru

crawl
クローゥ
ハイハイする
haihai suru

walk (baby talk)
ウォーク
あんよする（幼児語）
an-yo suru

stand (baby talk)
スタンド
たっちする（幼児語）
tacchi suru

WORDBANK — Babies 赤ちゃん

stroller	ストロウラァ	ベビーカー	bebiikaa
carry on one's back	キャリィ オン ワンズ バック	おんぶする	ombu suru
baby carrier	ベイビィ キャリアァ	抱っこひも	dakko himo
crib	クリブ	ベビーベッド	bebii beddo
crying at night	クライング アット ナイト	夜泣き	yonaki
heat rash	ヒート ラッシュ	あせも	asemo
diaper rash	ダイパァ ラッシュ	オムツかぶれ	omutsu kabure
vaccination	ヴァクシネイション	予防接種	yoboo sesshu
baby teeth	ベイビィ ティース	乳歯	nyuushi
baby food	ベイビィ フード	離乳食	rinyuushoku
bib	ビブ	よだれかけ	yodarekake
toilet training	トイレット トレイニング	オムツはずし	omutsu hazushi
wet one's pants	ウェット ワンズ パンツ	おもらしする	omorashi suru
wet one's bed	ウェット ワンズ ベッド	おねしょする	onesho suru

はじめよう／歩こう／買おう／食べよう／暮らそう／伝えよう／知っておこう

★Medical checkups are provided free of charge through the local government for children aged 1, 3-4, 6-7, 9-10, 12, 18, and 36 months. 1,3-4,6-7,9-10,12,18,36 ヵ月乳幼児検診が自治体によって無料で行われる

picky about food
ピキィ アバウト フード
食べ物の好き嫌いが多い
tabemono no sukikirai ga ooi

be shy around strangers
ビ シャイ アラウンド ストレインジャァズ
人見知りする
hitomishiri suru

selfish
セゥフィッシュ
わがままな
wagamama na

That's a good boy (girl)!
ザッツ ア グッド ボーイ(ガーゥ)
いい子ね!
Ii ko ne!

Mind your manners!
マインド ユアァ マナァズ
お行儀よくしなさい!
Ogyoogi yoku shinasai!

Good job!
グッド ジョブ
よくできたね!
Yoku dekita ne!

Control yourself!
コントローゥ ユアァセゥフ
我慢しなさい!
Gaman shinasai!

Let's play house!
レッツ プレイ ハウス
おままごとをしよう!
Omamagoto o shiyoo!

play make-believe
プレイ メイクビリーヴ
ごっこ遊びをする
gokko asobi o suru

picture coloring
ピクチャ カラリング
ぬり絵
nurie

picture book
ピクチャ ブック
絵本
ehon

hide-and-seek
ハイドアンドスィーク
かくれんぼ
kakurembo

fight
ファイト
けんかする
kenka suru

● Park パーァク 公園

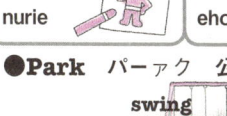

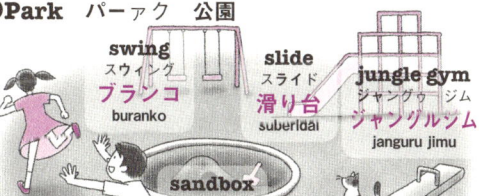

- swing スウィング ブランコ buranko
- slide スライド 滑り台 suberidai
- jungle gym ジャングゥ ジム ジャングルジム janguru jimu
- sandbox サンドボックス 砂場 sunaba
- tag タグ 鬼ごっこ onigokko
- see-saw スィーソー シーソー shiisoo

COLUMN
Parks/playspots
Since playgroups are relatively uncommon, mothers of small children go out and look for playmates for their children by visiting parks and childcare support centers. They also hope to make "*mamatomo*"—i.e., friends who have small children like their own.

公園・児童館
欧米によく見られるプレイグループは日本にあまりないので、乳幼児のいる親は児童館や子育て支援センターや公園など子供の遊び友達を探す。同じ年頃の子供をもつ親と「ママ友」になる目的も。

★Local governments offer "children's halls" as places for children to play. They have professional staff and put on a variety of activities. 子供たちの遊び場として自治体が設置しているのが「児童館」。専門職員がいてイベントも

Kindergarten / Nursery school

キンダァガーァトン/ナーァサリィ スクーゥ

幼稚園・保育園
Yoochien, hoikuen

Kindergarten
キンダァガーァトン

幼稚園
yoochien

Kindergartens are an educational facility. Children can attend after they turn 3, for 1-3 years. The standard kindergarten day is 4 hours.

教育施設のひとつ。満3歳以上の幼児を対象とし、学年単位で教育期間は1〜3年、1日4時間の保育が標準。

Nursery school
ナーァサリィ スクーゥ

保育園
hoikuen

Nursery schools ("hoikuen" or "hoikujo") offer daytime and/or evening care for working parents of preschool children.

保育所ともよばれる。保護者が働いている場合などに、昼間または夜間まで児童(0歳から就学前まで)を預かる。

When do you start accepting applications for next year?
ウェン ドゥ ユ スタートゥ アクセプティング アプリケイションズ フォァ ネクストゥ イヤァ

来年度の入園申し込みはいつからですか？

Rainendo no nyuuen mooshikomi wa itsukara desu ka?

application
アプリケイション

願書
gansho

Could you give me the necessary documents?
クジュ ギヴ ミ ザ ネセサリィ ダキュメンツ↑

必要な書類をいただけますか？

Hitsuyoona shorui o itadakemasu ka?

interview
インタヴュー

面接
mensetsu

Are there any openings here?
アァ ゼアァ エニィ オウプニング ヒアァ↑

こちらでは空きはありますか？

Kochira dewa aki wa arimasu ka?

No, we have a waiting list.
ノウ ウィ ハヴ ア ウェイティング リストゥ

いいえ。キャンセル待ちになります

Iie. Kyanseru machi ni narimasu.

What are your hours of operation?
ワットゥ アァ ユアァ アウァァズ オヴ オペレイション

何時から何時まで子供を預かってもらえますか？

Nanji kara nanji made kodomo o azukatte moraemasu ka?

pick up
ピック アップ

お迎えに行く
omukae ni iku

★Kindergartens and nursery schools often begin with an adjustment period, called "*narashi hoiku*," during which children are kept for only a short time. 多くの幼稚園・保育園では入園前に「慣らし保育」がある

Do children bring their own box lunches?
ドゥ チゥドレン ブリング ゼァア オウン バクス ランチズ↑

昼食はお弁当ですか？

Chuushoku wa obentoo desu ka?

Parent / guardian association
ペアレント／ガーディアン アソシエイション

保護者会

hogosha kai

We provide lunch 3 days a week.
ウィ プロヴァイド ランチ スリー デイズ ア ウィーク

週3回は給食です

Shuu sankai wa kyuushoku desu.

sports festival
スポーツ フェスティヴァゥ

運動会

undoo kai

---

excursion
イクスカーァジョン

遠足

ensoku

dance program
ダンス プログラム

お遊戯会

oyuugi kai

potato digging
ポテイトウ ディギング

芋堀り

imo hori

shellfish gathering
シェゥフィッシュ ギャザリング

潮干狩

shiohigari

● **Preschool activities**　園での活動

playing outside
プレイング アウトサイド
外遊び
sotoasobi

physical exercise
フィズィカゥ エクササイズ
体操
taisoo

singing songs
スィンギング ソングズ
歌を歌う
uta o utau

dance
ダンス
お遊戯
oyuugi

drawing
ドローイング
お絵かき
oekaki

arts and crafts
アーァツ アンド クラフツ
工作
koosaku

naptime
ナップタイム
お昼寝
ohirune

Have there been any changes?
ハヴ ゼァア ビン エニィ チェインジズ↑

何か変わったことはありますか？

Nanika kawatta koto wa arimasu ka?

He's (She's) fine.
ヒーズ（シーズ）ファイン

元気です

Genki desu.

He (She) has a slight cold.
ヒー（シー）ハズ ア スライト コウゥド

風邪気味です

Kaze gimi desu.

Someone was mean to him (her).
サムワン ワズ ミーン トゥ ヒム（ハァ）

意地悪されました

Ijiwaru saremashita.

He (She) fell.
ヒー（シー）フェゥ

転びました

Korobimashita.

★Some kindergartens and nursery schools offer "extended day care" for parents who cannot come by the specified closing time. 規定の保育終了時間に間に合わない場合に「延長保育」をする幼稚園・保育園も

87

School
スクーゥ

学校と行事
Gakko to gyooji

elementary school エレメンタリィ スクーゥ
小学校 shoogakkoo

4-year college フォーアイヤァ カリッジ
大学 daigaku

middle school ミドゥ スクーゥ
中学校 chuugakkoo

high school ハイ スクーゥ
高校 kookoo

technical school テクニカゥ スクーゥ
専門学校 semmon gakkoo

junior college ジュニアァ カリッジ
短期大学 tanki daigaku

public パブリック
公立 kooritsu

private プライヴェット
私立 shiritsu

academic year アカデミック イヤァ
学年 gakunen

class クラス
組 kumi

When does the academic year start?
ウェン ダズ ザ アカデミック イヤァ スターアト
学年度はいつ始まるのですか？
Gakunendo wa itsu hajimaru no desu ka?

principal プリンスィパゥ
校長 koochoo

It starts in April and ends in March.
イット スターアツ イン エイプリゥ アンド エンズ イン マーァチ
4月に始まって3月に終わります
Shigatsu ni hajimatte sangatsu ni owarimasu.

teacher in charge ティーチャァ イン チャーァジ
担任 tan-nin

COLUMN
Japanese school system
Children aged 6 as of April 1 enter elementary school. In Japan, compulsory education consists of 6 years of elementary school and 3 years of junior high school. After junior high, students can attend high school (3 years), then go on to technical school or college.

日本の学校制度
日本では4月1日時点で満6歳に達している児童が小学校に入学する。小学校は6年制、中学校は3年制で、日本国民はこの9年が義務教育。中学卒業後は希望により高等学校(3年制)や大学などに進学。

nurse's room ナーァスィズ ルーム
保健室 hokenshitsu

classroom クラスルーム
教室 kyooshitsu

library ライブラリィ
図書室 toshoshitsu

gym ジム
体育館 taiikukan

faculty room ファカゥティー ルーム
職員室 shokuinshitsu

playground プレイグラウンド
運動場 undoojoo

★ Elementary school students go to and from school in groups, called "*tōkōhan*," with the older children acting as leaders. 小学校では地域ごとの集団登下校がある。「登校班」では年長児童がリーダーに

How many class-hours are there per day?
ハウ メニィ クラスアウァーズ アァ ゼアァ パァ デイ

1日に何時間授業があるのですか？
Ichinichi ni nanjikan jugyoo ga aru no desu ka?

semester
セメスタァ
学期
gakki

Six hours.
スィクス アウァーズ
6時間ですよ
Rokujikan desuyo.

first semester
ファーアスト セメスタァ
1学期
ichigakki

second semester
セカンド セメスタァ
2学期
nigakki

third semester
サーアド セメスタァ
3学期
sangakki

What kind of events does this school have?
ワット カインド オヴ イヴェンツ ダズ ズィス スクーゥ ハヴ

この学校ではどんな行事がありますか？
Kono gakko dewa donna gyooji ga arimasu ka?

concert
カンサーアト
音楽会
ongakukai

cultural festival
カゥチュラゥ フェスティヴァゥ
文化祭
bunkasai

educational visit
エデュケイショナゥ ヴィズィット
社会科見学
shakaika kengaku

school trip
スクーゥ トリップ
修学旅行
shuugaku ryokoo

WORDBANK — School events 学校行事

entrance ceremony	エントランス セレモニィ	入学式	nyuugakushiki
graduation ceremony	グラデュエイション セレモニィ	卒業式	sotsugyooshiki
opening ceremony	オゥプニング セレモニィ	始業式	shigyooshiki
closing ceremony	クロウズィング セレモニィ	終業式	shuugyooshiki
evacuation drill	イヴァキュエイション ドリゥ	避難訓練	hinan kunren
sports day	スポーァツ デイ	体育祭	taiikusai
school festival	スクーゥ フェスティヴァゥ	学芸会	gakugeikai
class observation	クラス オゾァヴェイション	授業参観	jugyoo sankan

COLUMN
Public school districts
The public elementary and jr. high school a child attends is usually determined by the area he/she lives, called a "gakku (school district)." Recently, it has become more common to let children attend schools outside their district by adopting a "school selection system."

公立学校の学区
公立の小・中学校では、区域ごとに通学できる学校を指定している場合が多い。この区域を「学区」と呼ぶ。近年、学区外への通学を認める「学校選択制度」を実施する地域も増えてきた。

★Public school students in Japan are generally required to clean the classroom and school toilets after school. 日本の公立学校では、生徒が放課後にトイレや教室など校内を掃除するのが一般的だ

School life

スクーゥ ライフ
学校生活
Gakko seikatsu

> **Today he (she) will be absent due to a cold.**
> トゥデイ ヒー (シー) ウィゥ ビ アブセント デュー トゥ ア コウゥド
>
> 今日は風邪でお休みします
> Kyoo wa kaze de oyasumi shimasu.

> **Does he (she) have to take a ○○?**
> ダズ ヒー (シー) ハフ トゥ テイク ア ○○↑
>
> ○○を持っていく必要はありますか？
> ○○ o motteiku hitsuyoo wa arimasu ka?

WORDBANK — School items 持ち物

English	Katakana	Japanese	Romaji
backpack	バックパック	ランドセル	randoseru
name tag	ネイム タグ	名札	nafuda
school uniform	スクーゥ ユニフォーァム	制服	seifuku
gym shoes	ジム シューズ	運動靴	undoogutsu
indoor shoes	インドァ シューズ	上履き	uwabaki
gym clothes	ジム クロウズ	体操着	taisoogi
textbook	テクストブック	教科書	kyookasho
pen case	ペン ケイス	ふでばこ	fudebako
writing board	ライティング ボーァド	下敷き	shitajiki

money bag マニィ
集金袋
shuukin bukuro

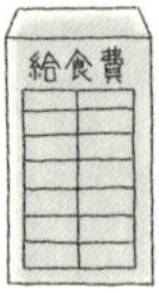

forget something フォアゲット サムスィング
忘れ物をする
wasuremono o suru

test テスト
テスト
tesuto

homework ホウムワァク
宿題
shukudai

report card リポーァト カァード
成績表
seisekihyoo

subject サブジェクト
教科
kyooka

~ period ピアリアド
～時間目
~ jikamme

WORDBANK — A day at school 学校の一日

English	Katakana	Japanese	Romaji
go to school	ゴウ トゥ スクーゥ	登校する	tookoo suru
bell	ベゥ	チャイム	chaimu
morning meeting	モーニング ミーティング	朝礼	choorei
break time	ブレイク タイム	休み時間	yasumijikan
lunch break	ランチ ブレイク	昼休み	hiruyasumi
leave school	リーヴ スクーゥ	下校する	gekoosuru
school-commute road	スクーゥコミュート ロゥド	通学路	tsuugakuro
after-school	アフタスクーゥ	放課後	hookago
club activities	クラブ アクティヴィティズ	クラブ活動	kurabu katsudoo

★Elementary school students wear a backpack called a "*randoseru*," which run for around 30,000 yen, with upscale brands costing even more. 小学生が背負う「ランドセル」は、平均3万円前後だが高級なブランド物も

home visit (by teacher)
ホウム ヴィズィット (バイ ティーチァ)

家庭訪問
katei hoomon

What is my child like at school?
ワット イズ マイ チャイゥド アット スクーゥ

うちの子は学校ではどうですか？
Uchi no ko wa gakko de wa doo desu ka?

individual interview
インディヴィデュアゥ インタヴュー

個人面談
kojin mendan

He (She) speaks up enthusiastically in class.
ヒー (シー) スピークス アップ エンシューズィアスティカリィ イン クラス

授業で積極的に発言していますよ
Jugyoo de sekkyokutekini hatsugen shite imasu yo.

Is my child keeping up with the lessons?
イズ マイ チャイゥド キーピング アップ ウィズ ザ レスンズ↑

うちの子は授業についていけていますか？
Uchi no ko wa jugyoo ni tsuiteikete imasu ka?

PTA meeting
ピーティーエー ミーティング

PTA総会
pii tii ee sookai

correspondence notebook
コレスポンデンス ノウトブック

連絡帳
renrakuchoo

The "correspondence notebook" is mainly used by teachers and parents to consult about studies, request absence from P.E., etc.

連絡帳は，主に小学校の教師と保護者との間で，勉強に関する相談や体育を休ませたいなどの事項を連絡するために使われる。

newsletter
ニューズレタァ

おたより
otayori

contact network
カンタクト ネットワーク

連絡網
renrakumoo

day duty
デイ デューティ

日直
nicchoku

Children take turns doing "day duty" at school. Their main tasks include saying "Stand" and "Bow," erasing the blackboard, and writing in the class journal.

日直は毎日児童が順番に担当。「起立，礼，着席」という号令かけ，黒板消し，学級日誌の記入などをする。

blackboard eraser
ブラックボード イレイサァ

黒板消し
kokubankeshi

blackboard
ブラックボード

黒板
kokuban

chalk
チョーク

チョーク
chooku

schedule
スケジューゥ

時間割
jikanwari

lunch monitor
ランチ マニタァ

給食当番
kyuushoku tooban

Lunch monitors alternate from week to week, and their job is carry lunch from the lunch room and serve it to the class. Each monitor wears a smock, a hat, and a mask.

給食当番は週ごとに児童数人が交代で担当。給食室から給食を運び，配膳する。白衣と帽子，マスクを着用。

attendance book
アテンダンス ブック

出席簿
shussekibo

teacher's desk
ティーチァズ デスク

教卓
kyootaku

tool box
トゥーゥ バクス

お道具箱
odoogubako

★Students usually wear school-designated gym clothes and room shoes. The school may even specify which stationery to use. 一般に体操着や上履きは学校指定のものを着用。その他文房具なども指定されている場合も

Company
カンパニィ
会社
Kaisha

I work at the head office.
アイ ワーァク アット ザ ヘッド アフィス

私は本社で働いています
Watashi wa honsha de hataraite imasu.

branch
ブランチ
支社
shisha

employee
インプロイー
従業員
juugyooin

joint-stock company
ジョイント スタック カンパニィ
株式会社
kabushiki gaisha

limited-liability company
リミティド ライアビリティィ カンパニィ
有限会社
yuugen gaisha

~ section
~ セクション
~ 課
~ ka

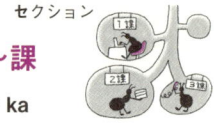

What department are you in?
ワット ディパーァトメント ァァ ユ イン

どこの部署で働いているんですか？
Doko no busho de hataraite irun desu ka?

general affairs
ジェネラゥ アフェアァズ
総務
soomu

The ○○ department.
ザ ○○ ディパーァトメント

○○部です
○○ bu desu.

public relations
パブリック リレイションズ
広報
koohoo

sales
セイゥズ
営業
eigyoo

accounting
アカウンティング
経理
keiri

human resources
ヒューマン リソーァスィズ
人事
jinji

development
ディヴェロップメント
開発
kaihatsu

employee training
インプロイー トレイニング
社員研修
shain kenshuu

client
クライアント
取引先
torihikisaki

subcontractor
サブカントラクタァ
下請け
shitauke

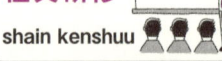

★Men are being encouraged to take childcare leave, but it is still uncommon.
男性の育児休暇も奨励されてはいるが、実際に育児休暇を取る男性はまだ多くない

●Job titles 役職

president
プレズィデント
社長
shachoo

vice-president
ヴァイス プレズィデント
副社長
fuku shachoo

department manager
ディパートメント マニジャァ
部長
buchoo

chief
チーフ
主任
shunin

section chief
セクション チーフ
係長
kakarichoo

section manager
セクション マニジャァ
課長
kachoo

COLUMN

"Nenkōjoretsu" is the system in which employees are promoted and paid based on seniority. Along with "lifetime employment," this is one of the pillars of the Japanese-style employment system; but in recent years companies have also started to adopt merit-based systems.

「年功序列」は、勤続年数や年齢に応じて昇進したり賃金が上がったりするシステム。従業員を定年まで雇い続ける「終身雇用」と並んでこれまでの日本型雇用の特徴だったが、最近では仕事の成果を評価して昇給・昇進を決める「成果主義」を併用する企業も。

---

boss
ボース
上司
jooshi

coworker
コウワーカァ
同僚
dooryoo

subordinate
サボーァディネット
部下
buka

I heard you're getting promoted next month.
アイ ハァード ユアァ ゲティング プロモウティド ネクスト マンス
あなた来月昇進するんだってね
Anata raigetsu shooshin surun datte ne.

be demoted
ビ ディモウティド
降格になる
kookaku ni naru

I got a raise!
アイ ガット ア レイズ
昇給があったんだ！
Shookyuu ga attanda!

take a pay cut
テイク ア ペイ カット
減給になる
genkyuu ni naru

---

monthly salary
マンスリィ サラリィ
月給
gekkyuu

bonus
ボウナス
ボーナス
boonasu

annual salary system
アニュアゥ サラリィ スィステム
年俸制
nempoosei

unaccompanied assignment
アナカンパニィド アサインメント
単身赴任
tanshin funin

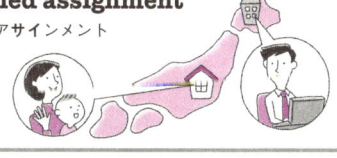

be transferred
ビ トランスファァド
転勤になる
tenkin ni naru

★ "Tanshin funin," a practice not seen much in other countries, is common in Japan.
ほかの国ではあまり見られないが、日本で単身赴任は一般的

Workplace etiquette

ワークプレイス エティケット

職場のルールとマナー
Shokuba no ruuru to manaa

Mind your appearance.
マインド ユアァ アピアランス
身だしなみに注意してください
Midashinami ni chuuishite kudasai.

Keep your desk area tidy.
キープ ユアァ デスク エリア タイディ
机周りを整理整頓してください
Tsukue mawari o seiri seiton shite kudasai.

clock in
クロック イン
タイムカードを押す
taimu kaado o osu

Always have your company ID on you.
オーゥウェイズ ハヴ ユアァ カンパニィ アイディー オン ユ
社員証を常に着用してください
Shain shoo o tsuneni chakuyoo shite kudasai.

be late
ビ レイト
遅刻する
chikokusuru

leave early
リーヴ アーァリィ
早退する
sootaisuru

notice of absence
ノウティス オヴ アブセンス
欠勤届
kekkin todoke

paid holiday
ペイド ハリデイ
有給休暇
yuukyuu kyuuka

absence without notice
アブセンス ウィザウト ノウティス
無断欠勤
mudan kekkinn

overtime allowance
オウヴァァタイム アラウアンス
残業手当
zangyoo teate

unpaid overtime
アンペイド オウヴァァタイム
サービス残業
saabisu zangyoo

I'd like to have the day off on 〜.
アイド ライク トゥ ハヴ ザ デイ オフ オン 〜
〜日にお休みをいただきたいのですが
〜 ni oyasumi o itadakitai no desu ga.

commute allowance
コミュート アラウアンス
通勤手当
tsuukin teate

Be sure to apply for holidays in advance.
ビ シュアァ トゥ アプライ フォァ ハリデイズ イン アドヴァンス
休暇は前もって申請するように
Kyuuka wa maemotte shinsei suru yooni.

★Smoke-free offices are also common in Japan.
日本でもオフィスは禁煙としているところが多い

I am ○○ of the sales department.
アイ アム ○○ オヴ ザ セィゥズ ディパートメント

営業部の○○と申します
Eigyoobu no ○○ to mooshimasu.

It's a pleasure to meet you.
イッツ ア プレジャァ トゥ ミート ユ

よろしくお願いします
Yoroshiku onegai shimasu.

●How to hold a business card　名刺の持ち方

Business cards are exchanged standing up. The "inferior" presents his/her card first, holding the card facing the recipient with both hands, keeping fingers clear of the print. It is also received with two hands.

名刺交換は立って行う。目下の者から先に渡す。渡すときは名刺を相手に向けて、文字に指がかからないように両手で持つ。受け取るときも両手で。

●Seating order in waiting rooms　応接室での席次

Clients and superiors sit in "upper seats," and hosts and lower-ranking people sit in "lower seats." In the diagram to the right, the numbers correspond to the person's rank. When serving tea, upper seat persons are served first.

目上の人やお客様が座るのが上座、目下の者や接待する側が座るのが下座。右図では①から順に上位の席。お茶を出す際は上座の人から順に出す。

●Positioning in elevators　エレベーターでの立ち位置

In the elevator as well, the "upper seat" is the position farthest from the door. The "lower seat" is the spot in front of the buttons. Avoid personal talk in the elevator, and if you exit before your boss or senior, say "*Osakini shitsureishimasu.*"

ドアから遠い奥が上座。操作ボタンの前が下座。私語は慎む。上司や先輩より先に降りる際は「お先に失礼します」と言う。

●Seating order in taxis/trains　タクシー・列車での席次

In taxis, the seating arrangement corresponds to rank as shown in the left diagram. In train compartments, the window seat facing forward is the upper seat.

タクシーでは、右図のように①から順に上位の席となる。列車のボックス席では進行方向を向いた窓側が上座となる。

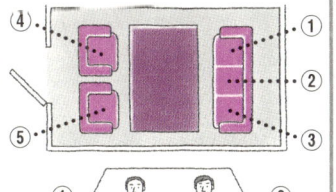

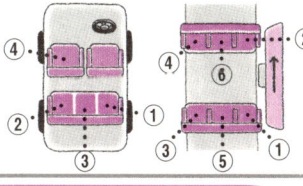

Thank you for your time.
サンキュ フォア ユアァ タイム

お忙しいところをどうもありがとうございました
Oisogashii tokoro o doomo arigatoo gozaimashita.

I look forward to working with you.
アイ ルック フォアワードゥ トゥ ワーァキング ウィズ ユ

今後ともよろしくお願いいたします
Kongotomo yoroshiku onegai itashimasu.

★In Japanese offices, people often keep their feelings about coworkers' appearance to themselves, so be careful how you look. 日本のオフィスでは、ほかの人の身だしなみが気になっても注意しないことが多い

Workplace talk

ワークプレイス
トーク

職場でのやり取り
Shokuba de no yaritori

Could you copy this for me?
クジュ カピィ ズィス フォア ミ↑

この書類をコピーしてくれる？

Kono shorui o kopiishite kureru?

Fax this map to ○○.
ファクス ズィス マップ トゥ ○○

この地図を○○にファックスしておいて

Kono chizu o ○○ ni fakkusu shite oite.

---

prepare a report
プリペァア ア リポーァト

報告書を作成する

hookokusho o sakusei suru

---

look over documents
ルック オウヴァア ダキュメンツ

資料に目を通す

shiryoo ni me o toosu

---

draw up a plan
ドゥロー アップ ア プラン

企画を立てる

kikaku o tateru

---

give a presentation
ギヴ ア プレゼンテイション

プレゼンする

purezen suru

---

have a meeting
ハヴ ア ミーティング

打合せ／会議する

uchiawase/kaigi suru

---

settle a bill with accounting
セトゥ ア ビゥ ウィズ アカウンティング

経費を精算する

keihi o seisan suru

Could you prepare some tea?
クジュ プリペア サム ティィ↑

お茶を入れてくれる？

Ocha o irete kureru?

Despite society's long-continuing advocacy of gender equality, it is still the job of women to serve tea to guests in many companies. Moreover, many offices still expect women to wipe desks and pour drinks at drinking parties.

男女平等が叫ばれて久しいが、来客があれば女性がお茶を出すことになっている会社は、今でも少なくない。机拭きや飲み会でのお酌などが女性に期待されることもまだ多い。

That job has to be finished by tomorrow.
ザット ジャブ ハス トゥ ビ フィニシュト バイ トゥモロウ

その仕事は必ず明日までに仕上げてくれ

Sono shigoto wa kanarazu asu made ni shiagete kure.

★ "Uchiawase" refers to preliminary meetings with a small number of people, whereas "kaigi" is used for formal meetings. 通常、少人数のミーティングを「打合せ」、形式ばったミーティングを「会議」とよぶ

●Whiteboard
ホワイトボード

田中	①直行
佐藤	②直帰
鈴木	③有休／年休
渡辺	④外出

①Visiting directly
ヴィズィティング ディレクトリィ
①直行
chokko

This means the person is going straight to the client, without stopping by the office.
職場に出勤せずに直接取引先などに出向くことを「直行」という。

②Going home directly
ゴウイング ホウム ディレクトリィ
②直帰
chokki

The person is going straight home after a client call, without returning to the office.
取引先などから、職場に戻ることなく直接帰宅することを「直帰」という。

③Paid holiday
ペイド ハリデイ
③有休／年休
yuukyuu/nenkyuu

"Annual paid holiday" (abbreviation of "*nenji yūkyū kyūka*.")
「年次有給休暇」を略して「有休」「年休」とよぶ。

④Out
アウト
④外出
gaishutsu

When leaving the office, write "外出," your destination, and return time.
職場から外出する場合は「外出」と書く。行き先や帰社時間を記すことも。

Is your work going smoothly?
イズ ユアァ ワーァク ゴウイング スムースリィ↑
仕事は順調に進んでる？
Shigoto wa junchoo ni susunderu?

quota
クウォウタ
ノルマ
noruma
田中／山田／小林

My work is ahead of schedule/behind schedule.
マイ ワーァク イズ アヘッド オヴ スケジューゥ／ビハインド スケジューゥ
私の仕事、予定より進んで／遅れてるの
Watashi no shigoto, yotei yori susunde/okurete runo.

●Greetings when leaving the office
退社時のあいさつ

Say "*Osakini shitsurei shimasu*" if your coworkers are still working when you leave the office, and "*Otsukaresama deshita*" to coworkers when they leave.

仕事中の同僚や上司を残して先に退社するときには「お先に失礼します」、先に退社する人に対しては、「お疲れさまでした」と声をかけよう。

Excuse me for leaving first.
イクスキューズ ミ フォァ リーヴィング ファーァスト
お先に失礼します
Osaki ni shitsurei shimasu.

Thank you for your hard work today.
サンキュ フォァ ユアァ ハーァド ワーァク トゥデイ
お疲れさまでした
Otsukaresama deshita.

Good, keep up the good work.
グッド キープ アップ ザ グッド ワーァク
ご苦労さまでした
Gokuroosama deshita.

"*Gokurōsamadeshita*" shows appreciation for the other person's labors, but is not used when speaking to a superior. Until recently, the same was true of "*otsukaresamadeshita*"; but now people commonly say this to their boss when leaving the office.

「ご苦労さまでした」は苦労をねぎらう言葉だが目上の人には言わない。元々は「お疲れさまでした」も同様だったが、現在は退社する上司に対して一般的に使われている。

★Workplace "*hōrensō*" refers to the "reporting (*hōkoku*)," "contact (*renraku*)," and "consultation (*sōdan*)" that are vital for smooth work operations. 仕事に重要な「報告・連絡・相談」を略して「ホウレンソウ」と言う

Taking phone calls, office supplies

テイキング フォウン コーゥズ アフィス サプライズ

電話応対・事務用品
Denwa ootai, jimuyoohin

○○ (company name).
○○ (カンパニィ ネイム)
○○（社名）でございます
○○ de gozaimasu.

This is ○○ of △△ (company name).
ズィス イズ ○○ オヴ △△ (カンパニィ ネイム)
△△（社名）の○○と申します
△△ no ○○ to mooshimasu.

COLUMN
At the office, try to pick up the phone by the third ring. If you can't, say "Sorry to keep you waiting" first.
会社での電話は3コール以内に出るように。それ以上待たせた場合は、最初に「お待たせしました」と言う。

Thank you for your support.
サンキュ フォア ユアァ サポーアト
お世話になっております
Osewa ni natte orimasu.

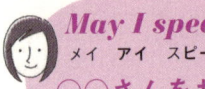

May I speak to ○○?
メイ アイ スピーク トゥ ○○↑
○○さんをお願いします
○○ o onegaishimasu.

One moment, please.
ワン モウメント プリーズ
少々お待ちください
Shooshoo omachikudasai.

○○ is away from his desk right now.
○○ イズ アウェイ フロム ヒズ デスク ライト ナウ
○○はただいま席をはずしております
○○ wa tadaima seki o hazushite orimasu.

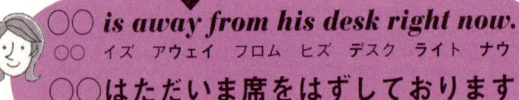

with a visitor
ウィズ ア ヴィズィタァ
来客中で
raikyakuchuu de

I'm sorry, may I have your name again, please?
アイム サリィ メイ アイ ハヴ ユアァ ネイム アゲン プリーズ↑
恐れ入りますが、お名前をもう一度お願いします
Osoreirimasu ga, onamae o mooichido onegai shimasu.

in a meeting
イン ア ミーティング
会議中で
kaigichuu de

on another line	**out of the office**	**call back**
オン アナザァ ライン	アウト オヴ ズィ アフィス	コーゥ バック
ほかの電話に出て	外出中で	（電話を）かけ直す
hokano denwa ni dete	gaishutsuchuu de	kakenaosu

★Personal phone calls and internet use are generally prohibited at the workplace.
私用電話は禁止職場での私用電話や使用のインターネット利用は通常禁止されている

○○ should be back at ~.
○○ シュド ビ バック アット ~

○○は~時に戻る予定です
○○ wa ~ ji ni modoru yotei desu.

fixtures
フィクスチャア
備品
bihin

office equipment
アフィス イクウィプメント
オフィス機器
ofisu kiki

We're out of ○○. Take care of it.
ウィアァ アウト オヴ ○○ テイク ケアァ オヴ イット

○○がなくなってるよ。補充しておいて
○○ ga nakunatteru yo. Hojuu shite oite.

locker
ラカァ
ロッカー
rokkaa

copy paper
カーピィ ペイパァ
コピー用紙
kopii yooshi

fax
ファクス
ファックス
fakkusu

copier
カーピアァ
コピー機
kopiiki

correction fluid
コレクション フルイド
修正液
shuusei eki

PC
ピースィー
パソコン
pasokon

calculator
カゥキュレイタァ
電卓
dentaku

chair
ナェアァ
いす
isu

transparent file
トランスペアレント ファイゥ
クリアファイル
kuriafairu

payment slip
ペイメント スリップ
支払伝票
shiharai dempyoo

invoice
インヴォイス
請求書
seikyuu sho

Post-it
ポゥスティット
付箋
husen

eraser
イレイサァ
消しゴム
keshigomu

desk
デスク
机
tsukue

stapler
ステイプラァ
ホッチキス
hocchikisu

The copy machine is out of order.
ザ カーピィ マシーン イズ アウト アヴ オーァダァ

コピー機が故障しました
Kopiiki ga koshoo shimashita.

call the repairman
コーゥ ザ リペアァマン
サービスマンを呼ぶ
saabisu man o yobu

★Be aware that taking supplies out of the office is a crime.
職場の備品の持ち出しは犯罪になるので要注意

Bank, post office
バンク ポウスト アフィス

銀行・郵便局
Ginkoo, yuubinkyoku

I'd like to open a regular savings account.
アイド ライク トゥ オウプン ア レギュラァ セイヴィング アカウント

普通預金の口座を開きたいのですが
Futsuu yokin no kooza o hirakitai no desu ga.

Please take a number and wait.
プリーズ テイク ア ナンバァ アンド ウェイト

そちらの番号札をお取りになってお待ちください
Sochira no bangoo fuda o otori ni natte omachi kudasai.

term deposit
ターァム ディパズィット

定期預金
teiki yokin

We need a passport or some other form of identification.
ウィ ニード ア パスポート オァア サム アザァ フォーム オヴ アイデンティフィケイション

パスポートなどご本人様確認書類が必要です
Pasupooto nado gohon-ninsama kakunin shorui ga hitsuyoo desu.

interest rate
インタレスト レイト

利率
riritsu

fee
フィー

手数料
tesuuryoo

automatic withdrawal
オートマティック ウィズドゥローァゥ

自動引き落とし
jidoo hikiotoshi

exchange rate
イクスチェインジ レイト

為替レート
kawase reeto

installment savings
インストーゥメント セイヴィング

積立預金
tsumitate yokin

foreign remittance
フォーリン リミッタンス

海外送金
kaigai sookin

I'd like to change some foreign currency.
アイド ライク トゥ チェインジ サム フォーリン カレンスィ

外貨の両替をしたいのですが
Gaika no ryoogae o shitai no desu ga.

★A seal is usually required for opening a bank account, but some banks accept a signature.
通常銀行口座開設には印鑑が必要だが、サインで口座開設できる銀行もある

WORDBANK — Bank 銀行

English	カタカナ	日本語	Romaji
ATM card	エイティーエム カーァド	キャッシュカード	kyasshu kaado
withdrawal	ウィズドゥローアゥ	引出し	hikidashi
deposit	ディパズィット	預入れ	azukeire
payment (into an account)	ペイメント (イントゥ アン アカウント)	振込み	furikomi
PIN	ピン	暗証番号	anshoo bangoo
bankbook entry	バンクブック エントリィ	通帳記入	tsuuchoo kinyuu
balance inquiry	バランス インクワイァリィ	残高照会	zandaka shookai
investment trust	インヴェストメント トラスト	投資信託	tooshi shintaku

mortgage モーァギッジ
住宅ローン
juutaku roon

lend レンド
貸し付ける
kashitsukeru

I'd like to send this by ○○.
アイド ライク トゥ センド ズィス バイ ○○
これを○○で送りたいのですが
Kore o ○○ de okuritai no desu ga.

What is it?
ワット イズ イット
中身は何ですか？
Nakami wa nan desu ka?

express mail イクスプレス メイゥ
速達
sokutatsu

air mail エアァ メイゥ
航空便
kookuu bin

sea mail スィー メイゥ
船便
funa bin

registered mail レジスタァド メイゥ
書留
kakitome

courier service クリアァ サーァヴィス
宅配便
takuhai bin

Transport companies and the post office have courier services. They will even come to your door to pick up a parcel, at no extra cost. Deliveries can also be made from convenience stores.

運送会社や郵便局で。通常荷物1つでも無料で集荷。コンビニでも発送可能。

delivery notice デリヴァリィ ノウティス
不在連絡票
tuzai renraku hyoo

If you are not at home when a parcel or registered item is delivered, you will get a "delivery notice." Re-delivery appointments can be made by phone or internet.

宅配便や書留などの配達時に留守の場合「不在連絡票」が届く。電話やネットを通して再配達を依頼できる。

WORDBANK — Mail 郵便

English	カタカナ	日本語	Romaji
mailbox	メイゥバクス	ポスト	posuto
letter	レタァ	封書	fuusho
postcard	ポウストカーァド	ハガキ	hagaki
stamp	スタンプ	切手	kitte
payment on delivery	ペイメント オン デリヴァリィ	着払い	chakubarai
cash on delivery	キャッシュ オン デリヴァリィ	代引き	daibiki
Express Mail Service	イクスプレス メイゥ サーァヴィス	EMS	iiemuesu
Surface Air Lifted	サーァフィス エアァ リフティド	SAL	saru
delivery certificate	デリヴァリィ サーァティフィケット	配達証明	haitatsu shoomei

★Public utility bill payments can be made not only at banks and post offices but also at most convenience stores. 公共料金などの振り込みは、郵便局・銀行のほか多くのコンビニでもできる

Government offices

ガヴァメント アフィスィズ
役所
Yakusho

Do I need to sign up for ○○?
ドゥ アイ ニード トゥ サイン アップ フォア ○○↑
○○に加入する必要はありますか？
○○ ni kanyuu suru hitsuyoo wa arimasu ka?

National Pension
ナショナゥ ペンション
国民年金
kokumin nenkin

All Japanese residents aged 20-60 are, regardless of nationality, required to take out a National Pension policy.

日本の公的年金で、日本に住所のある20歳以上60歳未満のすべての人が、国籍を問わずに加入を義務付けられている。

Nursing Care Insurance
ナーァスィング ケアァ インシュアランス
介護保険
kaigo hoken

Insurance provided to certain people aged 40-65 and all people over 65 who need nursing care. People 40 and over are required to pay premiums.

40歳以上の特定疾患要介護者、65歳以上の要介護者にサービスを提供する。満40歳以上が保険料を支払う。

National Health Insurance
ナショナゥ ヘゥス インシュアランス
国民健康保険
kokumin kenkoo hoken

Taken out by people over 20 who do not have health insurance through their company or a mutual aid association. Premiums vary by income and local government policy.

会社の健康保険や公務員の共済組合に入っていない20歳以上の該当者が対象。保険料は収入や自治体で異なる。

I lost my health insurance card.
アイ ロスト マイ インシュアランス カーァド
保険証をなくしてしまいました
Hoken shoo o nakushite shimaimashita.

I'd like to apply for alien registration.
アイド ライク トゥ アプライ フォア エイリアン レジストレイション
外国人登録の申請をしたいのですが
Gaikokujin tooroku no shinsei o shitai no desu ga.

Certificate of Registered Matters
サーァティフィケット オヴ レジスタァド マタァズ
登録原票記載事項証明書
tooroku gempyoo kisaijikoo shoomei sho

Issued as proof of alien registration items such as residence, date of birth, nationality, type of visa, status, etc., it serves the same function as a Japanese person's certificate of residence. To request it at a government office, an alien registration card or other ID is required.

居住地や生年月日、国籍、在留資格など、外国人登録の登録事項の証明として発行され、日本人の住民票と同じ役割を果たす。役所で請求する際は本人確認資料が必要。

window
ウィンドウ
窓口
madoguchi

★ The types of social welfare facilities and services offered vary, so check with your local government.
保養所や福祉サービスなどは自治体によってさまざまなので、確認してみよう

seal registration
スィーゥ レジストレイション

印鑑登録
inkan tooroku

Registration of a seal at a government office, for identification purposes. A "seal registration certificate" is required for home purchases.

身分証明用に役所に自分の印鑑を登録する。「印鑑登録証明書（印鑑証明）」は不動産購入時などに必要。

I'd like a seal certification.
アイド ライク ア スィーゥ サーァティフィケイション

印鑑証明が欲しいのですが
Inkan shoomei ga hoshii no desu ga.

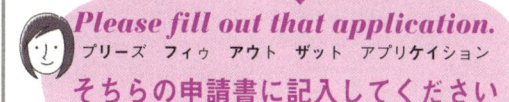

Please fill out that application.
プリーズ フィゥ アウト ザット アプリケイション

そちらの申請書に記入してください
Sochira no shinsei sho ni kinyuu shite kudasai.

medical expense subsidy
メディカゥ イクスペンス サブサディィ

医療費助成
iryoohi josei

Local governments offer a medical expense subsidy for young children who often need medical attention. Some places offer a subsidy until the aged of 15.

自治体では通院の機会の多い乳幼児の医療費助成を行っている。15歳まで助成を延長している自治体もある。

child allowance
チャイゥド アラウアンス

子ども手当
kodomo teate

What documents do I need to submit a birth notice?
ワット ダキュメンツ ドゥ アイ ニード トゥ サブミット ア バースス ノウティス

出生届を出すのに必要な書類は何ですか？
Shusshoo todoke o dasu no ni hitsuyoona shorui wa nan desu ka?

You need a proof of birth form, your maternity handbook, and your seal.
ユ ニード ア プルーフ オヴ バースス フォーァム ユアァ マタァニティィ ハンドブック アンド ユアァ スィーゥ

出生証明書、母子手帳、印鑑が必要です
Shusshoo shoomei sho, boshi techoo, inkan ga hitsuyoo desu.

residential tax
レズィデンシャゥ タクス

住民税
juumin zei

fail to pay
フェイゥ トゥ ペイ

滞納する
tainoosuru

welfare benefits
ウェゥフェアァ ベネフィッツ

生活保護
seikatsu hogo

I'd like to consult with someone about ○○.
アイド ライク トゥ コンサゥト ウィズ サムワン アバウト ○○

○○について相談したいのですが
○○ ni tsuite soodan shitai no desu ga.

★Many local government offices have English- and Chinese-speaking staff on hand to answer all kinds of questions. 多くの自治体では、英語や中国語を話すスタッフが各種の相談に応じるサービスを行っている

Seeing a doctor

スィーイング ア ダクタァ

診察の予約・健康診断
Shinsatsu no yoyaku, kenkoo shindan

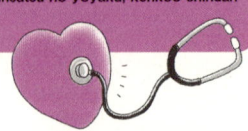

I'd like to make an appointment.
アイド ライク トゥ メイク アン アポイントメント

診察の予約をしたいのですが
Shinsatsu no yoyaku o shitai no desu ga.

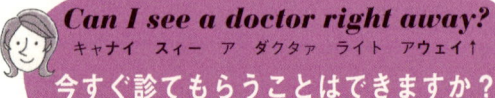

Can I see a doctor right away?
キャナイ スィー ア ダクタァ ライト アウェイ↑

今すぐ診てもらうことはできますか？
Imasugu mite morau koto wa dekimasu ka?

Can you introduce me to a doctor who speaks English?
キャン ユ イントロデュース ミ トゥ ア ダクタァ フー スピークス イングリッシュ↑

英語を話せるお医者様を紹介してもらえませんか？
Eigo o hanaseru oishasama o shookai shite moraemasen ka?

---

hospital
ハスピタゥ
病院
byooin

clinic
クリニック
医院／診療所
iin/shinryoojo

usual/main doctor
ユージュアゥ／メイン ダクタァ
かかりつけ／主治医
kakaritsuke/shujii

I'd like to make an appointment for my daughter's 3-month check-up.
アイド ライク トゥ メイク アン アポイントメント フォア マイ ドータァズ スリー マンス チェカップ

娘の3カ月検診の予約をお願いします
Musume no sankagetsu kenshin no yoyaku o onegai shimasu.

---

first medical exam
ファーァスト メディカゥ イグザム
初診
shoshin

hospital card
ハスピタゥ カーァド
診察券
shinsatsuken

WORDBANK — Medical care 医療

internal physician	インターァナゥ フィズィシャン	内科医	naikai
pediatrician	ピディアトリシャン	小児科医	shoonikai
dentist	デンティスト	歯科医	shikai
surgeon	サーァジョン	外科医	gekai
ENT doctor	イーエヌティー ダクタァ	耳鼻科医	jibikai
ophthalmologist	アフサゥマラジスト	眼科医	gankai
dermatologist	ダァマタロジスト	皮ふ科医	hifukai
psychiatrist	サイキアトリスト	精神科医	seishinkai
obstetrician	オブステトリシャン	産科医	sankai

★Doctors are addressed with the honorific "-*sensei*" (not "-*san*").
医師に呼びかける場合は、「○○さん」などではなく「先生」と言おう

Do you give medical checkups?
ドゥ ユ ギヴ メディカゥ チェカップス↑

そちらで健康診断は受けられますか？
Sochira de kenkoo shindan wa ukeraremasu ka?

Yes, it costs ¥ ~ .
イェス イット コスツ ~ イェン

はい、費用は~円かかります
Hai, hiyoo wa ~ en kakarimasu.

COLUMN

As a rule, businesses pay for workers' medical checkups. Voluntary checkups are not covered by insurance.

労働者の健康診断の費用は事業者負担が原則。任意で受ける場合は保険適用外となるため高額になる。

medical sheet
メディカゥ シート

問診票
monshin hyoo

We need to do another exam, with an endoscope.
ウィ ニード トゥ ドゥ アナザァ イグザム ウィズ アン エンドスコウプ

内視鏡で再検査が必要です
Naishikyoo de saikensa ga hitsuyoo desu.

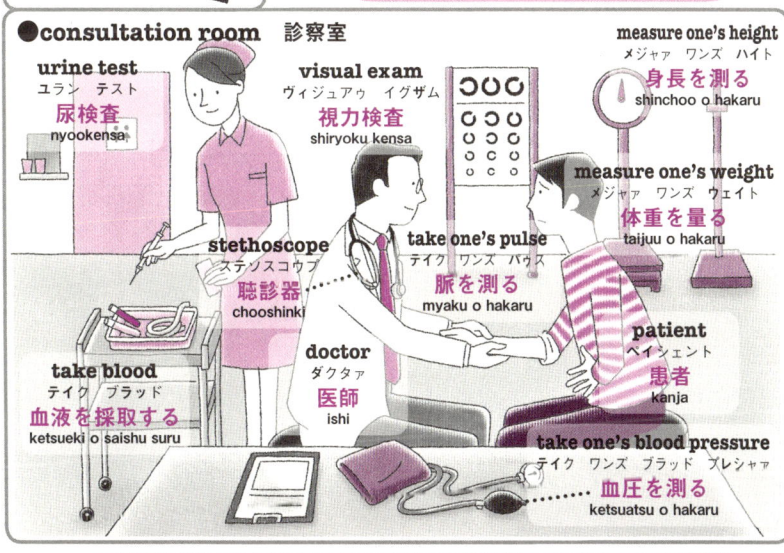

● **consultation room** 診察室

urine test
ユラン テスト
尿検査
nyookensa

visual exam
ヴィジュアゥ イグザム
視力検査
shiryoku kensa

measure one's height
メジャァ ワンズ ハイト
身長を測る
shinchoo o hakaru

stethoscope
ステソスコウプ
聴診器
chooshinki

take one's pulse
テイク ワンズ パゥス
脈を測る
myaku o hakaru

measure one's weight
メジャァ ワンズ ウェイト
体重を量る
taijuu o hakaru

take blood
テイク ブラッド
血液を採取する
ketsueki o saishu suru

doctor
ダクタァ
医師
ishi

patient
ペイシェント
患者
kanja

take one's blood pressure
テイク ワンズ ブラッド プレシャァ
血圧を測る
ketsuatsu o hakaru

I'd like to have my teeth checked and cleaned.
アイド ライク トゥ ハヴ マイ ティース チェックト アンド クリーンド

歯のチェックとクリーニングをお願いします
Ha no chekku to kuriiningu o onegai shimasu.

★People aged 40-74 who are covered by public medical insurance are eligible for a health check for detecting metabolic syndrome. 40〜74歳の公的医療保険加入者に、「メタボ健診」が実施されている

Beauty salon, barber shop
ビューティ サロン バーバァ シャップ

美容院・理髪店
Biyooin, rihatsuten

I'd like to make a reservation.
アイド ライク トゥ メイク ア リザヴェイション

予約をお願いしたいのですが
Yoyaku o onegai shitai no desu ga.

For when?
フォア ウェン

いつがご希望ですか？
Itsu ga gokiboo desu ka?

Tomorrow at 11 o'clock, please.
トゥモロウ アット イレヴン オクラック プリーズ

明日の11時にお願いします
Asu no juuichiji ni onegai shimasu.

hairdresser
ヘアァドレサァ
美容師
biyooshi

Would you like anyone in particular?
ウジュ ライク エニワン イン パァティキュラァ↑

指名はございますか？
Shimei wa gozaimasu ka?

hairstyle
ヘアァスタイゥ
ヘアスタイル
heasutairu

○○, please.
○○ プリーズ

○○さんにお願いできますか？
○○ san ni onegai dekimasu ka?

Anyone is fine.
エニワン イズ ファイン

誰でも結構です
Dare demo kekko desu.

shampoo
シャンプー
シャンプー
shampuu

What can I do for you today?
ワット キャナイ ドゥ フォア ユ トゥデイ

今日はいかがされますか？
Kyoo wa ikaga saremasu ka?

blow-dry
ブロウドライ
ブロー
buroo

A haircut and perm, please.
ア ヘアァカット アンド パーァム プリーズ

カットとパーマをお願いします
Katto to paama o onegai shimasu.

★Hairdressers and barbers have different licenses. For a shave, go to a barber.
美容師と理容師は別々の資格。ひげそりは理髪店で

I'd like to have my hair conditioned.
アイド ライク トゥ ハヴ マイ ヘアァ コンディションド
トリートメントしてください
Toriitomento shite kudasai.

dyed
ダイド
染めて
somete

straightened
ストレイトゥンド
ストレートパーマをかけて
sutoreeto paama o kakete

Please make it look like this photo.
プリーズ メイク イット ルック ライク ズィス フォウトウ
この写真のようにしてください
Kono shashin no yooni shite kudasai.

loose perm
ルース パーァム
ゆるいパーマ
yurui paama

tight perm
タイト パーァム
強いパーマ
tsuyoi paama

layered out
レイヤァド カット
レイヤーカット
reiyaa katto

single-length
スィングゥ レングス
ワンレングス
wanrengusu

dreadlocks
ドレッドロックス
ドレッド
doreddo

close-cropped
クロウスクラップト
丸刈り
marugari

crew cut
クルー カット
クルーカット
kuruukatto

shave
シェイヴ
ひげそり
higesori

Just cut the ends in a straight line, please.
ジャスト カット ズィ エンズ イン ア ストレイト ライン プリーズ
毛先を揃えるだけにしてください
Kesaki o soroeru dake ni shite kudasai.

thin out one's hair
スィン アウト ワンズ ヘアァ
髪をすく
kami o suku

Please thin out the bangs.
プリーズ スィン アウト ザ バングズ
前髪を軽くしてください
Maegami o karuku shite kudasai.

set one's hair
セット ワンズ ヘアァ
髪をセットする
kami o setto suru

Please cut the sides a little more.
プリーズ カット ザ サイズ ア リトゥ モアァ
サイドをもう少しカットしてください
Saido o moo sukoshi katto shite kudasai.

put one's hair up
プット ワンズ ヘアァ アップ
髪をアップにする
kami o appu ni suru

★Discount barber shops at stations and shopping malls that offer 10 minute haircuts for 1,000 yen are on the rise. 駅構内やショッピングモールなどで、「10分1000円」といった格安スピードカットの店が増えてきた

Getting Understood
伝えよう

Abbreviations 短縮語

Japanese people like to shorten words when they talk.
日本人は、ことばを略して話すのが好き。

あけおめ ことよろ
→明けましておめでとう 今年もよろしく
"Ake ome. Koto yoro" is "Akemashite omedetou. Kotoshi mo yoroshiku."

ときとば
→時と場合による
"Tokitoba" is "toki to baai ni yoru."

まんきつ
→漫画喫茶
"Mankitsu" is "manga kissa."

ぱねえ
→半端じゃない
"Panee" is "hanpa janai."

That 4-beat rhythm is catchy. Even people's names get shortened.
やっぱり4拍のリズムが気持いい。人名でも品名でも、バンバン略す！

リモコン
"リモートコントローラー
"Rimokon" is "remote control."

キムタク
"木村拓哉
"Kimutaku" is "Kimura Takuya."

マツジュン
"松本潤
"Matsujun" is "Matsumoto Jun."

エアコン
"エアーコンディショナー
"Eakon" is "air conditioner."

As for my friend "Mori Kurumi"...
ちなみに・・・友人の「もりくるみ」ちゃん。みんなに

もりくる
"Morikuru"
is what they call her.
って呼ばれてた。

あと一文字なのに…
That's practically the whole name.

Empty invitations 社交辞令

Japanese person A: 今度飲みにいきましょう！
Let's go drinking sometime!

Japanese person B: 引越したの。遊びにきてね〜
I just moved. Come and visit me!

ちょっと待ったー
Wait!

日本人が気軽に言うこれらはたいていその気がなく、別れ際になんとなく言っているだけなので本気にしないで

Japanese people say these things casually, but usually they don't really mean it. They're just empty parting words, so don't take them seriously.

そうなの？
Really?

Kyoto is notorious for this. If you're at someone's home and they say,
有名なのが京都。他人宅を訪問したときの

ぶぶ漬でも（お茶漬）どうですか？
Would you care for some "bubu zuke (rice and tea)"?

This means, "You've been here long enough that I'm obliged to serve you a light meal, so it's about time you left."
これは、「軽い食事を出すくらい時間が経った。そろそろ帰ってくれないかな」という意味です。

むずかしーっ
So complicated!

京都の都市伝説ニャ。これは日本人でもムズかしいニャー

This is a Kyoto urban legend. Even Japanese find it complicated.

Time

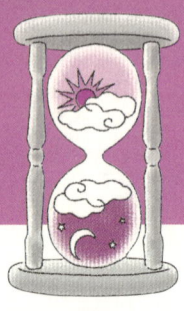

タイム
時間
Jikan

What time is it?
ワット タイム イズ イット

今、何時ですか？
Ima, nanji desu ka?

How long will it take?
ハウ ロング ウィゥ イット テイク

どれぐらい(時間)かかりますか？
Doregurai kakarimasu ka?

early morning	morning		A.M.		noon
アーァリィ モーァニング	モーァニング		エイエム		ヌーン
早朝 soochoo	朝 asa		午前 gozen		昼 hiru

12 a.m.	2 a.m.	4 a.m.	6 a.m.	8 a.m.	10 a.m.	12 p.m.
トウェゥヴ エイエム	トゥー エイエム	フォーァ エイエム	スィクス エイエム	エイト エイエム	テン エイエム	トウェゥヴ ピーエム
0時 reiji	2時 niji	4時 yoji	6時 rokuji	8時 hachiji	10時 juuji	12時 juu niji

| 0時 | 1時 | 2時 | 3時 | 4時 | 5時 | 6時 | 7時 | 8時 | 9時 | 10時 | 11時 | 12時 |

1 a.m.	3 a.m.	5 a.m.	7 a.m.	9 a.m.	11 a.m.
ワン エイエム	スリー エイエム	ファイヴ エイエム	セヴン エイエム	ナイン エイエム	イレヴン エイエム
1時 ichiji	3時 sanji	5時 goji	7時 shichiji	9時 kuji	11時 juu ichiji

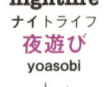

nightlife
ナイトライフ
夜遊び
yoasobi

sunrise
サンライズ
日の出
hinode

get up
ゲット アップ
起床
kishoo

breakfast
ブレックファスト
朝食
chooshoku

go to school
ゴウ トゥ スクーゥ
登校
tookoo

go to work
ゴウ トゥ ワーァク
出勤
shukkin

early
アーァリィ
早い
hayai

right on time
ライト オン タイム
時間ぴったり
jikan pittari

late
レイト
遅刻
chikoku

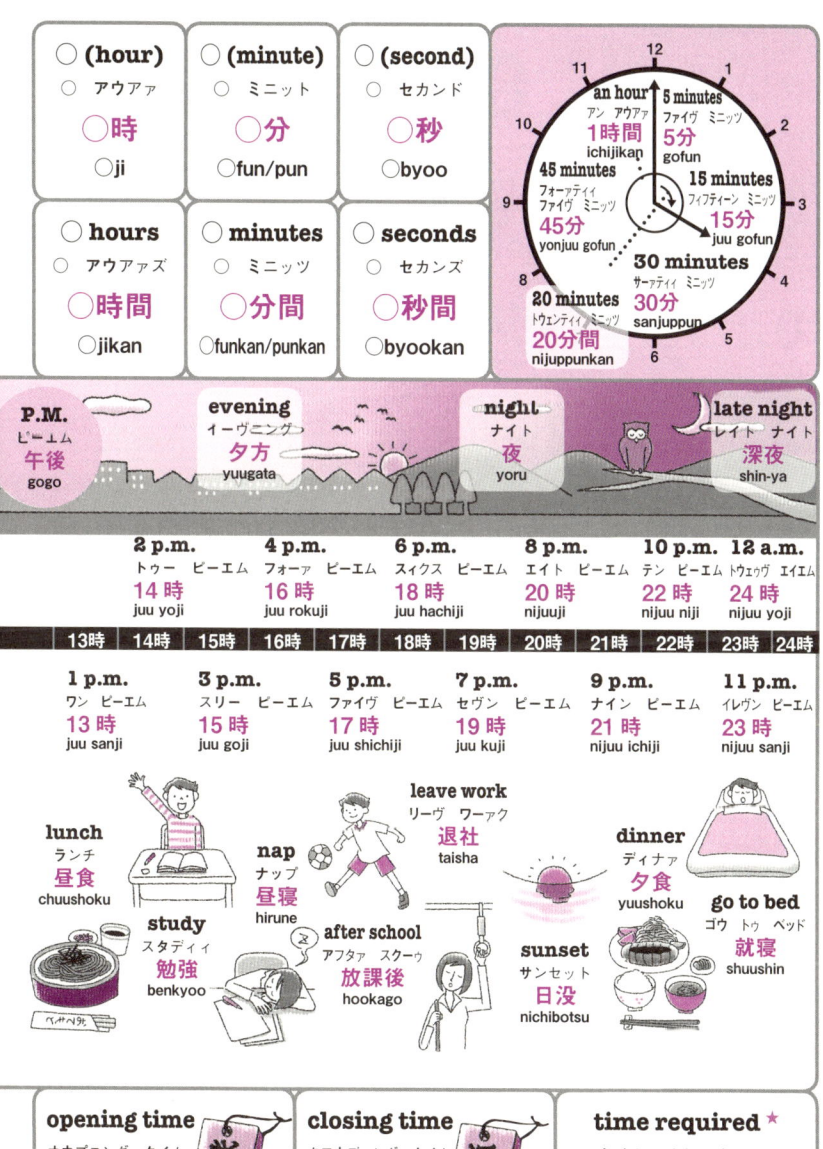

○ (hour)	○ (minute)	○ (second)
アウァァ	ミニット	セカンド
○時	○分	○秒
○ji	○fun/pun	○byoo

○ hours	○ minutes	○ seconds
アウァァズ	ミニッツ	セカンズ
○時間	○分間	○秒間
○jikan	○funkan/punkan	○byookan

an hour / アン アウァァ / 1時間 / ichijikan
5 minutes / ファイヴ ミニッツ / 5分 / gofun
45 minutes / フォーティヴ ファイヴ ミニッツ / 45分 / yonjuu gofun
15 minutes / フィフティーン ミニッツ / 15分 / juu gofun
30 minutes / サーティイ ミニッツ / 30分 / sanjuppun
20 minutes / トウェンティィ ミニッツ / 20分間 / nijuppunkan

P.M. ピーエム 午後 gogo
evening イーヴニング 夕方 yuugata
night ナイト 夜 yoru
late night レイト ナイト 深夜 shin-ya

2 p.m.	4 p.m.	6 p.m.	8 p.m.	10 p.m.	12 a.m.
トゥー ピーエム	フォー ピーエム	スィクス ピーエム	エイト ピーエム	テン ピーエム	トゥウェヴ エイエム
14時	16時	18時	20時	22時	24時
juu yoji	juu rokuji	juu hachiji	nijuuji	nijuu niji	nijuu yoji

| 13時 | 14時 | 15時 | 16時 | 17時 | 18時 | 19時 | 20時 | 21時 | 22時 | 23時 | 24時 |

1 p.m.	3 p.m.	5 p.m.	7 p.m.	9 p.m.	11 p.m.
ワン ピーエム	スリー ピーエム	ファイヴ ピーエム	セヴン ピーエム	ナイン ピーエム	イレヴン ピーエム
13時	15時	17時	19時	21時	23時
juu sanji	juu goji	juu shichiji	juu kuji	nijuu ichiji	nijuu sanji

lunch ランチ 昼食 chuushoku
nap ナップ 昼寝 hirune
leave work リーヴ ワーァク 退社 taisha
dinner ディナァ 夕食 yuushoku
study スタディィ 勉強 benkyoo
after school アフタァ スクーゥ 放課後 hookago
sunset サンセット 日没 nichibotsu
go to bed ゴゥ トゥ ベッド 就寝 shuushin

opening time	closing time	time required ★
オウプニング タイム	クロウズィング タイム	タイム リクワイアァド
開店時間	閉店時間	所要時間 ★
kaiten jikan	heiten jikan	shoyoo jikan

★How long it takes to do something is often noted as *shoyoo* ○*fun* (Required: ○ min.).
所要時間とは目的を成しとげるためにかかる時間のこと。所要○分という使い方をする

Numbers

ナンバァズ
数字
Suuji

0.1 rei ten ichi	**one-tenth** ワンテンス	
十 juu	**ten** テン	
百 hyaku	**hundred** ハンドレッド	
千 sen	**thousand** サウザンド	
万 man	**ten thousand** テン サウザンド	
十万 juuman	**hundred thousand** ハンドレッド サウザンド	
百万 hyakuman	**million** ミリアン	
億 oku	**hundred million** ハンドレッド ミリアン	

0	零 rei/zero	**zero** ズィアロウ	
1	一 ichi	**one** ワン	
2	二 ni	**two** トゥー	
3	三 san	**three** スリー	
4	四 shi/yon	**four** フォーァ	
5	五 go	**five** ファイヴ	
6	六 roku	**six** スィクス	
7	七 nana/shichi	**seven** セヴン	
8	八 hachi	**eight** エイト	
9	九 ku/kyuu	**nine** ナイン	

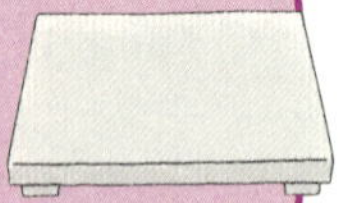

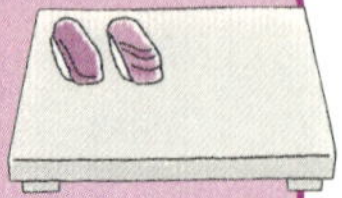

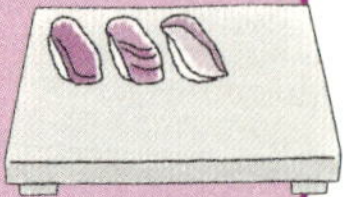

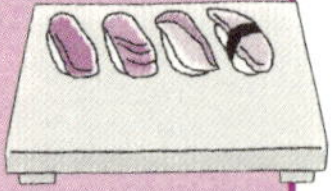

はじめよう / 歩こう / 買おう / 食べよう / 暮らそう / 伝えよう / 知っておこう

10 ten juu テン	◯ 人 ◯ people ◯ nin ◯ ピープゥ	◯ 個 ◯ items ◯ ko ◯ アイテムズ
11 eleven juu ichi イレヴン	◯ 回 ◯ times ◯ kai ◯ タイムズ	◯ 冊 ◯ books ◯ satsu ◯ ブックス
22 twenty-two nijuu ni トゥエンティィ トゥー	◯ 階 ◯ floors ◯ kai ◯ フローァズ	◯ 皿 ◯ plates ◯ sara ◯ プレイツ
333 three hundred and thirty-three sambyaku sanjuu san スリー ハンドレッド アンド サーァティィ スリー	◯ 台 ◯ vehicles ◯ dai ◯ ヴィークゥズ	◯ 匹 ◯ animals ◯ hiki/biki ◯ アニマゥズ
4分の1 one-fourth yombun no ichi ワンフォーァス	◯ 枚 ◯ flat objects ◯ mai ◯ フラット アブジクツ	◯ 本 ◯ long objects ◯ hon/pon/bon ◯ ロング アブジクツ
0.5＝1/2、半分 five-tenths, one half, or half rei ten go = nibun no ichi, hambun ファイヴ テンス ワン ハーフ オーァ ハーフ	◯ 〜目 number ◯ in a series (3rd, 4th, etc.) （例：3個目、4回目） ◯ me (rei: sankome, yonkome) ナンバァ ◯ イン ア スィアリーズ (サーァド フォーァス エトセトラ)	
6倍 six times rokubai スィクス タイムズ	いくつ必要ですか？ How many do you need? Ikutsu hitsuyoo desu ka? ハウ メニィ ドゥ ユ ニード	
7等分 divided into seven equal parts nanatoobun ディヴァイディド イントゥ セヴン イークヮゥ パーァツ	いくらですか？ How much is this? Ikura desu ka? ハウ マッチ イズ ズィス	
8000円 ¥8,000 hassen-en エイト サウザンド イェン		
全部 all zembu オーゥ		

COLUMN

In Japanese, various counter suffixes are added after numbers when describing quantities. Houses are counted in *ken*, chairs in *kyaku*, and fish in *bi*. There used to be 500 such suffixes, but people are less careful about them now. Some versatile counters such as *ko*, *hiki*, and *hon* can be used for many different things. But don't use the animal counter *hiki* to count people!

数の後につけてものの数量をあらわす助数詞の種類が多いのが日本語の特徴だ。家は1軒、イスは1脚、魚は1尾のように、数える対象によって異なった助数詞が適用される。古くは500種類を超えるというが、近年ではあまり意識して使うことが少なくなっており、「個」「匹」「本」など多数の言葉に兼用される助数詞も多い。ただし、人が1匹、犬が1人などの間違いはしないようにしたい。

Year, month, date, day

イヤァ マンス デイト デイ

年月日・曜日
Nengappi, yoobi

When did you arrive in Japan?
ウェン ディデュ アライヴ イン ジャパン

いつ日本に来ましたか？

Itsu nihon ni kimashita ka?

yesterday
イェスタァデイ

昨日

kinoo

the day before yesterday
ザ デイ ビフォア イェスタァデイ

おととい

ototoi

today
トゥデイ

今日

kyoo

When do you go back home?
ウェン ドゥ ユ ゴウ バック ホウム

いつ故郷へ帰りますか？

Itsu kokyoo e kaerimasu ka?

tomorrow
トゥマロウ

明日

ashita

the day after tomorrow
ザ デイ アフタァ トゥマロウ

あさって

asatte

three days from now
スリー デイズ フラム ナウ

しあさって

shiasatte

COLUMN

Chinese zodiac signs
十二支について

Time and space were once described using the sexagenary cycle. 10 "stems" and 12 "branches" (from ancient Chinese yin and yang cosmology) are the framework for years, months, days, hours, and directions. After a cycle of 60 combinations, one returns to the start. That's why 60th birthdays are significant. Names of animals are used to remember the 12 branches. Even today, one's birth year is associated with animals and their traits. Also used in fortune-telling.

古代中国伝来の陰陽五行説をもとにしたのが十干十二支。干支はこれを組み合せ、年、月、日、時刻、方角などの時間と空間を秩序づけたもの。組合せは60通りあり、一巡すると元に還る。還暦がこれにあたる。十二支には動物が割り当てられ、子年、丑年など、今でも生まれ年を動物で表し、運勢占いに利用される。

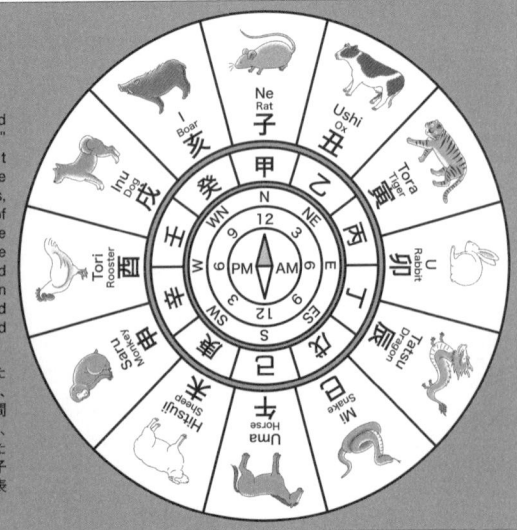

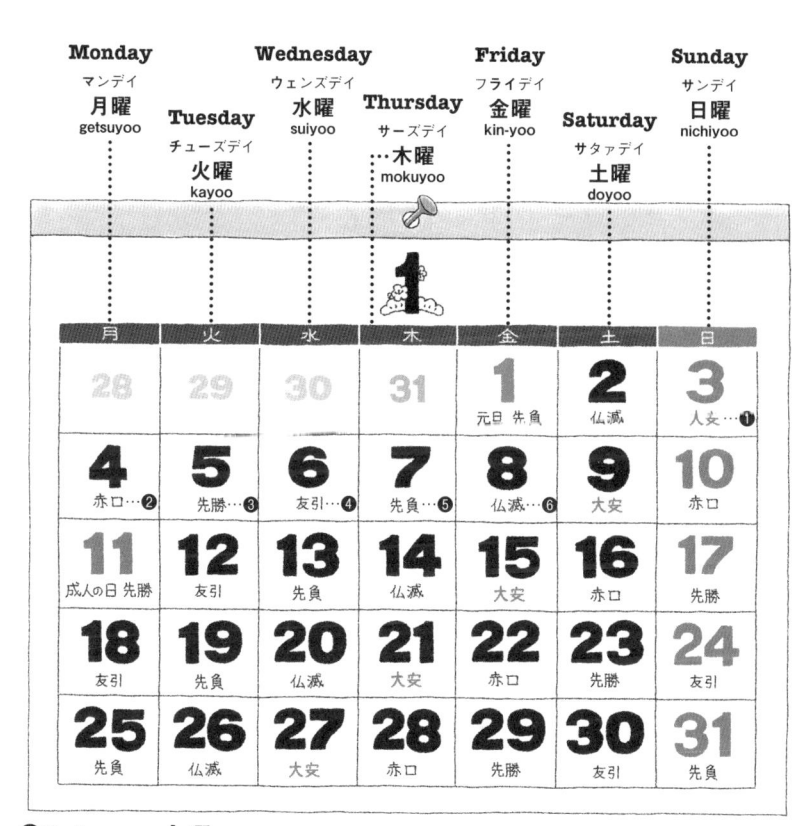

Monday	Tuesday	Wednesday	Thursday	Friday	Saturday	Sunday
マンデイ	チューズデイ	ウェンズデイ	サーズデイ	フライデイ	サタァデイ	サンデイ
月曜 getsuyoo	火曜 kayoo	水曜 suiyoo	木曜 mokuyoo	金曜 kin-yoo	土曜 doyoo	日曜 nichiyoo

月	火	水	木	金	土	日
28	29	30	31	1 元日 先負	2 仏滅	3 大安 … ❶
4 赤口 … ❷	5 先勝 … ❸	6 友引 … ❹	7 先負 … ❺	8 仏滅 … ❻	9 大安	10 赤口
11 成人の日 先勝	12 友引	13 先負	14 仏滅	15 大安	16 赤口	17 先勝
18 友引	19 先負	20 仏滅	21 大安	22 赤口	23 先勝	24 友引
25 先負	26 仏滅	27 大安	28 赤口	29 先勝	30 友引	31 先勝

●Rokuyo 六曜

A cycle of six lucky and unlucky days throughout the year, based on traditional Japanese fortune-telling called *onmyodo*.

陰陽道（日本の古くからの占い）で吉や凶を決める基準となる6つの日を指す。

❶ Taian 大安

Good luck in general. Chosen for weddings and other ceremonies.

万事によいとされる日。結婚式などはこの日を選ぶことが多い

❷ Shakko / Shakku 赤口

Bad luck in general. People avoid starting lawsuits, official events, and contracts.

すべてに凶とされる日。特に訴訟や公事、契約などは避ける

❸ Senshoo 先勝

Good luck in the morning. A good day for urgent business. Bad luck in the afternoon.

午前中は吉。急用にもよい日。この日の午後は凶

❹ Tomobiki 友引

Competing is not advised. Good luck in the morning and evening. Bad for funerals because *tomobiki* means "dragging friends along".

朝夕は吉、昼は凶。「友を引く」というところから葬式は避ける

❺ Senbu 先負

Bad luck in the morning, but good luck in the afternoon. Not a good day for urgent business or official events.

午前は凶、午後は吉。急用、公式の行事にはよくない日

❻ Butsumetsu 仏滅

Bad luck in general. Avoid weddings, opening new stores, and other ceremonies.

万事に凶であるとされる日。結婚式や店の開店などは避けたほうがよいとされる

Body, physical condition

バディ フィズィカゥ コンディション
体・体調
Karada, taichoo

What's wrong?
ワッツ ロング
どうしたの？
Dooshitano?

My stomach hurts.
マイ スタマック ハーァツ
おなかが痛いんだ
Onaka ga itainda.

My ○○ hurts.
マイ ○○ ハーァツ
○○が痛いです
○○ ga itai desu.

I don't feel good.
アイ ドゥント フィーゥ グッド
気分が悪いです
Kibun ga warui desu.

I feel drained.
アイ フィーゥ ドレインド
だるいんです
Daruin desu.

I feel nauseous.
アイ フィーゥ ノーシャス
吐き気がします
Hakike ga shimasu.

I have a fever.
アイ ハヴ ア フィーヴァァ
熱があります
Netsu ga arimasu.

I have a cough.
アイ ハヴ ア コフ
咳が出ます
Seki ga demasu.

I have a runny nose.
アイ ハヴ ア ラニィ ノウズ
鼻水が出ます
Hanamizu ga demasu.

I have a chill.
アイ ハヴ ア チゥ
寒気がします
Samuke ga shimasu.

I don't have any appetite.
アイ ドゥント ハヴ エニィ アペタイト
食欲がありません
Shokuyoku ga arimasen.

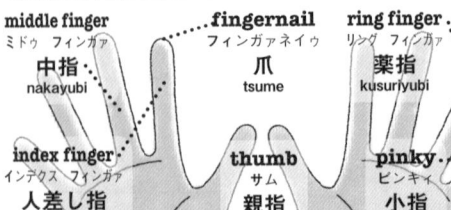

---

middle finger ミドゥ フィンガァ 中指 nakayubi
fingernail フィンガァネイゥ 爪 tsume
ring finger リング フィンガァ 薬指 kusuriyubi
index finger インデクス フィンガァ 人差し指 hitosashiyubi
thumb サム 親指 oyayubi
pinky ピンキィ 小指 koyubi
left hand レフト ハンド 左手 hidarite
finger フィンガァ 指 yubi
right hand ライト ハンド 右手 migite

diarrhea ダイアリーア 下痢 geri

constipation カンスティペイション 便秘 bempi

★The cedar and cypress pollen-induced hay fever season starts at the end of the year and lasts through early May. スギやヒノキによる花粉症は、年末ごろから5月初旬ごろまで続く

●Body 身体

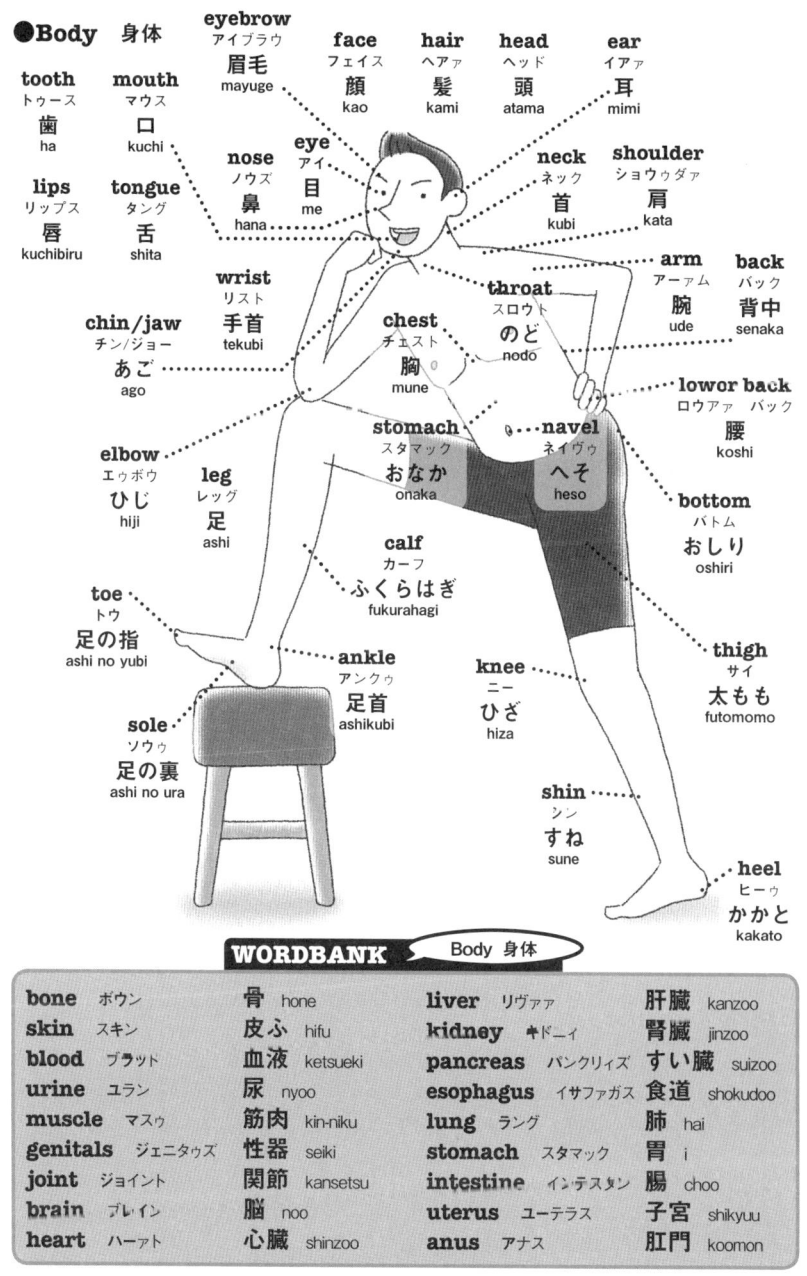

- **eyebrow** アイブラウ 眉毛 mayuge
- **face** フェイス 顔 kao
- **hair** ヘアァ 髪 kami
- **head** ヘッド 頭 atama
- **ear** イアァ 耳 mimi
- **tooth** トゥース 歯 ha
- **mouth** マウス 口 kuchi
- **nose** ノウズ 鼻 hana
- **eye** アイ 目 me
- **neck** ネック 首 kubi
- **shoulder** ショウゥダァ 肩 kata
- **lips** リップス 唇 kuchibiru
- **tongue** タング 舌 shita
- **wrist** リスト 手首 tekubi
- **throat** スロウト のど nodo
- **arm** アーァム 腕 ude
- **back** バック 背中 senaka
- **chin/jaw** チン/ジョー あご ago
- **chest** チェスト 胸 mune
- **stomach** スタマック おなか onaka
- **navel** ネイヴゥ へそ heso
- **lower back** ロウアァ バック 腰 koshi
- **elbow** エゥボウ ひじ hiji
- **leg** レッグ 足 ashi
- **bottom** バトゥム おしり oshiri
- **calf** カーフ ふくらはぎ fukurahagi
- **toe** トウ 足の指 ashi no yubi
- **ankle** アンクゥ 足首 ashikubi
- **knee** ニー ひざ hiza
- **thigh** サイ 太もも futomomo
- **sole** ソウゥ 足の裏 ashi no ura
- **shin** シン すね sune
- **heel** ヒーゥ かかと kakato

WORDBANK — Body 身体

bone	ボウン	骨	hone
skin	スキン	皮ふ	hifu
blood	ブラッド	血液	ketsueki
urine	ユラン	尿	nyoo
muscle	マスゥ	筋肉	kin-niku
genitals	ジェニタゥズ	性器	seiki
joint	ジョイント	関節	kansetsu
brain	ブレイン	脳	noo
heart	ハーァト	心臓	shinzoo
liver	リヴァァ	肝臓	kanzoo
kidney	キドゥニィ	腎臓	jinzoo
pancreas	パンクリィズ	すい臓	suizoo
esophagus	イサファガス	食道	shokudoo
lung	ラング	肺	hai
stomach	スタマック	胃	i
intestine	インテスタン	腸	choo
uterus	ユーテラス	子宮	shikyuu
anus	アナス	肛門	koomon

Illnesses, injuries
イゥネスィズ インジュリィズ
病気・けが
Byooki, kega

Please take me to the hospital.
プリーズ テイク ミ トゥ ザ ハスピタゥ
病院へ連れていってください
Byooin ni tsurete itte kudasai.

Is there an emergency hospital nearby?
イズ ゼアァ アン イマーァジェンスィィ ハスピタゥ ニアァバイ↑
近くに救急病院はありますか？
Chikaku ni kyuukyuu byooin wa arimasu ka?

---

patient reception
ペイシェント リセプション
診療受付
shinryoo uketsuke

outpatient
アウトペイシェント
外来
gairai

waiting room
ウェイティング ルーム
待合室
machiaishitsu

be admitted into a hospital
ビ アドミティド イントゥ ア ハスピタゥ
入院する
nyuuin suru

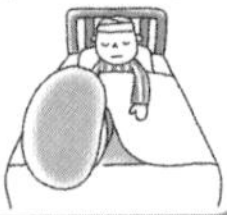

thorough testing
サーロウ テスティング
精密検査
seimitsu kensa

surgery
サーァジェリィ
手術
shujutsu

I hurt my leg.
アイ ハーァト マイ レッグ
足をけがしました
Ashi o kega shimashita.

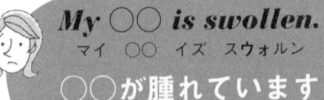

My ○○ is swollen.
マイ ○○ イズ スウォルン
○○が腫れています
○○ ga harete imasu.

---

sterilize
ステラライズ
消毒する
shoodoku suru

shot
シャット
注射
chuusha

WORDBANK — Injuries けが

burn	バーァン	やけど	yakedo
sprain	スプレイン	ねんざ	nenza
blow	ブロウ	打撲	daboku
bone fracture	ボウン フラクチャァ	骨折	kossetsu
dislocation	ディスロケイション	脱臼	dakkyuu
bleeding	ブリーディング	出血	shukketsu
wound	ウーンド	傷口	kizuguchi
cast	キャスト	ギプス	gipusu
anesthesia	アネスィージャ	麻酔	masui

★The Bureau of Health and Social Welfare has a hotline introducing medical facilities in English, Chinese, Korean, Spanish, and Thai. 東京都福祉保険局は、英・中・韓・スペイン・タイ語で医療機関を紹介している

I'm going to look at your throat. Open your mouth, please.
アイム ゴウイング トゥ ルック アット ユアァ スロウト オウブン ユアァ マウス ブリーズ

喉を見ます。お口を開けてください

Nodo o mimasu. Okuchi o akete kudasai.

Please show me your tummy.
ブリーズ ショウ ミ ユアァ タミィ

おなかを見せてください

Onaka o misete kudasai.

Does it hurt when I press here?
ダズ イット ハーァト ウェン アイ ブレス ヒアァ↑

ここを押すと痛みますか

Koko o osuto itamimasu ka?

Take care.
テイク ケアァ

お大事に

Odaiji ni.

allergy アラァジィ **アレルギー** arerugii	**asthma** アスマ **喘息** zensoku	**the flu** ザ フルー **インフルエンザ** infuruenza	**cold** コウゥド **風邪** kaze

gastroenteritis ガストロウエンテライタス
胃腸炎 ichooen

I'm going to give you a prescription.
アイム ゴウイング トゥ ギヴ ユ ア ブリスクリプション

処方箋を出しますね

Shohoosen o dashimasu ne.

WORDBANK — Diagnoses 病名

anemia アニーミア	貧血	hinketsu
high blood pressure ハイ ブラッド プレシャァ	高血圧	kooketsuatsu
low blood pressure ロウ ブラッド プレシャァ	低血圧	teiketsuatsu
nasal inflammation ネイザゥ インフラメイション	鼻炎	bien
hay fever ヘイ フィーヴァァ	花粉症	kahun shoo
indigestion インダイジェスチョン	消化不良	shooka furyoo
food poisoning フード ポイズニング	食中毒	shokuchuudoku
heatstroke ヒートストロウク	熱中症	necchuu shoo
tooth decay トゥース ディケイ	虫歯	mushiba

2 tablets at a time
トゥー タブレッツ アット ア タイム

1回2錠

ikkai nijou

before/after meals
ビフォーァ／アフタァ ミーゥズ

食前／食後

shokuzen/shokugo

★Drugs prescribed at clinics are bought at pharmacies that take prescriptions. See p. 48 for drug names.
診療所で処方された薬は処方箋を受け付ける薬局で買う。薬の名称はP.48参照

Worries
ウォリィズ
心配ごと
Shimpai goto

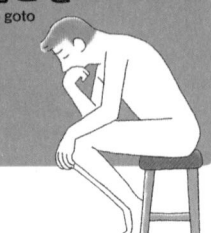

You look down.
ユ ルック ダウン

浮かない顔をしているね
Ukanai kao o shiteiru ne.

I'm suffering from ○○.
アイム サファリング フロム ○○

○○に悩んでいるんだ
○○ ni nayande irunda.

I'm worried about ～.	lonely	feel depressed
アイム ウォリィド アバウト ～	ロウンリィ	フィーゥ ディプレスト
～が心配だ	**さびしい**	**気がめいる**
～ ga shimpai da.	sabishii	ki ga meiru

I'm worn out from looking after my kids.
アイム ワーン アウト フロム ルッキング アフタァ マイ キッズ

育児にもう疲れたわ
Ikuji ni moo tsukareta wa.

What's wrong? Talk to me.
ワッツ ロング トーク トゥ ミ

どうしたの？ 私に話して
Dooshita no? Watashi ni hanashite.

COLUMN

Local governments offer counseling on school, housing, work, and other issues, so if you have a problem, try visiting your local government office first. For health issues, talk to your local public health center, and for childcare issues, talk to the home support center.

自治体では、学校や住まい、就職などさまざまな問題に対応する相談窓口を設けているので、困ったことがあったらまずは自治体にあたってみよう。また、健康に関することなら地域の保健センターに、育児に関することなら子ども家庭支援センターに相談しよう。

lack of sleep	insomnia
ラック オヴ スリープ	インソムニア
睡眠不足	**不眠症**
suimin busoku	fumin shoo

depression	be irritated
ディプレション	ビ イリテイティド
うつ病	**イライラする**
utsu byoo	iraira suru

★ "Hikikomori", or social withdrawal, is not just a Japanese problem; it is also becoming more common in the West. 「引きこもり」は日本だけでなく欧米でも増えてきている

Work is stressing me out.
ワーァク イズ ストレスィング ミ アウト

仕事のストレスがたまっているんです
Shigoto no sutoresu ga tamatte irundesu.

I have no motivation to do anything.
アイ ハヴ ノウ モティヴェイション トゥ ドゥ エニスィング

何もやる気が起きません
Nani mo yaru ki ga okimasen.

No one understands.
ノウ ワン アンダスタンズ

誰もわかってくれないんです
Dare mo wakatte kurenaindesu.

You shouldn't think about it too much.
ユ シュドゥント スィンク アバウト イット トゥー マッチ

考えすぎないほうがいいよ
Kangaesuginai hoo ga ii yo.

Things will work out.
スィングズ ウィゥ ワーァク アウト

なんとかなるよ
Nantoka naruyo.

My child is being bullied at school.
マイ チャイゥド イズ ビーイング ブリィド アット スクーゥ

子どもが学校でいじめられているようです
Kodomo ga gakkoo de ijimerarete iru yoo desu.

My boss is sexually harrassing me.
マイ バス イズ セクシャリィ ハラスィング ミ

上司からのセクハラに困っています
Jooshi kara no sekuhara ni komatte imasu.

Why don't you try talking to ○○?
ワイ ドウンチュ トライ トーキング トゥ ○○

○○に相談してみたら？
○○ ni soodan shite mitara?

power harrassment
パワァ ハラスメント

パワハラ
pawahara

---

physically abuse ~
フィズィカリィ アビューズ ~

～に暴力を振るう
~ ni booryoku o furuu

have an affair
ハヴ アン アフェアァ

浮気する
uwakisuru

get homesick
ゲット ホウムスィック

ホームシックになる
hoomushikku ni naru

★Victims of child abuse who refuse to go to school have become a social problem.
家庭での児童虐待で、不登校になる子どもが社会問題になっている

Accidents and problems
アクスィデンツ アンド プラブレムズ

事故・トラブル
Jiko, toraburu

I lost my camera.
アイ ロスト マイ キャメラ

カメラをなくしました
Kamera o nakushimashita.

My wallet was stolen.
マイ ワレット ワズ ストウルン

財布を盗まれました
Saifu o nusumare mashita.

passport	suitcase	luggage	handbag
パスポート	スーツケイス	ラギッジ	ハンバッグ
パスポート	スーツケース	荷物	ハンドバッグ
pasupooto	suutsu keesu	nimotsu	hando baggu

cancel a credit card
キャンセゥ ア クレディット カァード

クレジットカードを無効にする
kurejitto kaado o mukoo ni suru

report a theft
リポァート ア セフト

盗難届を出す
toonan todoke o dasu

Is there anyone who understands English?
イズ ゼァア エニワン フー アンダスタンズ イングリッシュ↑

英語がわかる人はいますか？
Eigo ga wakaru hito wa imasu ka?

I'd like to contact the embassy (consulate).
アイド ライク トゥ カンタクト ズィ エンバスィィ（カンシュレット）

大使館（領事館）に連絡したいのですが
Taishikan (Ryoojikan) ni renraku shitai no desu ga.

Calm down.	**Don't worry.**	**It's all right.**
カーム ダウン	ドゥント ウォリィ	イッツ オーゥ ライト
落ち着いて	心配しないで	大丈夫ですよ
Ochitsuite.	Shimpai shinaide.	Daijjoobu desu yo.

★Dial 110 for emergency law enforcement service and 119 for fire or ambulance service.
警察への緊急通報は110番、火災や救急の場合は119番に電話する

purse-snatching	**pickpocketing**	**groping**
パース スナチング	ピックパケティング	グロウピング
ひったくり	スリ	痴漢
hittakuri	suri	chikan

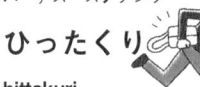

I had a traffic accident.	**be swindled**
アイ ハド ア トラフィック アクスィデント	ビ スウィンドゥド
交通事故にあいました	詐欺にあう
Kootsuu jiko ni aimashita.	sagi ni au.

Stop! Robber!
スタップ ラバァ
待て！ どろぼう！
Mate! Doroboo!

Stop it!
スタップ イット
やめて！
Yamete!

Help!
ヘゥプ
助けて！
Tasukete!

Catch him/her!
キャッチ ヒム/ハァ
捕まえて！
Tsukamaete!

Call the police(ambulance)!
コーゥ ザ ポリース（アンビュランス）
警察（救急車）を呼んで！
Keisatsu(Kyuukyuusha) o yonde!

Go away!
ゴウ アウェイ
あっちへ行って！
Acchi e itte!

Watch out!	**Let go!**	**Get out!**
ワッチ アウト	レット ゴウ	ゲット アウト
危ない！	離して！	出て行け！
Abunai!	Hanashite!	Dete ike!

Fire! Call the fire department!
ファイアァ コーゥ ザ ファイアァ ディパァトメント
火事だ！ 消防車を呼んで！
Kajida! Shooboo sha o yonde!

earthquake
アーァスクウェイク
地震
jishin

★Japan is not as safe as it used to be. Beware of bicycle basket bag-snatchers and unlit streets at night.
日本も治安が悪いところが増えてきた。自転車カゴからのひったくり、暗い夜道などには気をつけて

Clothing/Shoes Conversion Table 衣服・靴のサイズ対照表

※Size displays vary by country. Note that standards also vary slightly by maker/type of clothing.
　サイズは、国によって表示が異なる。また、メーカーや服の種類によって若干規格が違うことも多いので注意しよう

Men's Clothing (suits, coats, sweaters, etc.) 紳士服（スーツ・コート・セーターなど）

Japan 日本	S		M		L		LL
US/UK 米・英	34	36	38	40	42	44	46
Europe 欧	44	46	48	50	52	54	56

Men's Shirts (neck) 紳士ワイシャツ（首周り）

Japan/Europe 日・欧	36	37	38	39	40	41	42
US/UK 米・英	14	14.5	15	15.5	16	16.5	17

Men's Shoes 紳士靴

Japan 日本	24	24.5	25	25.5	26	26.5	27
US 米	6	6.5	7	8	8.5	9	9.5
UK 英	5.5	6	6.5	7	7.5	8	8.5
Europe 欧	38	39	40	41	42	43	44
Japan 日本	27.5	28	28.5	29	29.5	30	30.5
US 米	10	10.5	11	11.5	12	12.5	13
UK 英	9	9.5	10	10.5	11	11.5	12
Europe 欧	45	46	47	48	49	50	51

Men's Socks 紳士靴下

Japan 日本	24	24.5	25	25.5	26	26.5	27	27.5
US/UK 米・英	9		9.5		10		10.5	
Europe 欧	38		39		40		41	
Japan 日本	28	28.5	29	29.5	30	30.5		
US/UK 米・英	11			11.5				
Europe 欧	42			43				

Women's Clothing (suits, coats, etc.) 婦人服（スーツ・コートなど）

Japan 日本	5	7	9	11	13	15	17
US 米	6	8	10	12	14	16	18
Australia 豪	10	12	14	16	18	20	22
UK 英	30	32	34	36	38	40	42
Europe 欧	34	36	38	40	42	44	46

Women's Shoes 婦人靴

Japan 日本	22	22.5	23	23.5	24	24.5	25
US 米	5	5.5	6	6.5	7	7.5	8
UK 英	3.5	4	4.5	5	5.5	6	6.5
Europe 欧	34	35	36	37	38	39	40
Japan 日本	26	26.5	27	27.5	28		
US 米	9	9.5	10	10.5	11		
UK 英	7	7.5	8	8.5	9		
Europe 欧	40.5	41	41.5	42	42.5		

Women's Hosiery 婦人靴下・ストッキング

Japan 日本	22	22.5	23	23.5	24	24.5	25	25.5	26	26.5
US/UK 米・英	9				9.5			10		10.5
France/Germany 仏・独	2			3				4		5
Europe 欧	37				38			39		40

Tips for enjoying conversation in Japan
会話を楽しむための基本情報が満載

Getting Proficient
知っておこう

Facts & Figures ——————————————— 126
日本の基礎データと度量衡換算表

Learn more about Japan ——————————— 128
日本にまつわる雑学ガイド

Useful expressions ——————————————— 134
簡単ひとことフレーズ講座

Vocabulary list ————————————————— 136
アルファベット順日本語単語帳

Facts & Figures 日本の基礎データと度量衡換算表

Japan 日本国

Japan at a Glance 国のあらまし

Area	面積	377,944 km² (as of 2008)	37万7944 km² (2008年)
Population	人口	127,076,200 (as of 2009)	約1億2707万6200人 (2009年)
National Flower	国花	Cherry blossom	桜
Capital	首都	Tokyo (Pop. 12,548,300 as of 2009)	東京 (人口約1254万8300人、2009年)
Language	公用語	Japanese	日本語

Traveling in Japan 旅のヒント

【Currency】
The yen comes in ¥1,000, ¥2,000, ¥5,000, and ¥10,000 notes and ¥1, ¥5, ¥10, ¥50, ¥100, and ¥500 coins. USD $1 = ¥93, €1 = ¥113, AUD$1 = ¥79 (Jun 2010)

【Electricity】
100 V, 50/60 Hz. A transformer and adapter may be needed when using home appliances. Japan uses type A plugs.

【Mail】
Stamps can be bought at post offices and convenience stores. It costs ¥70 to send a postcard overseas. Regular mail postage varies depending on size and destination. Mailboxes are red and can be readily found.

【通貨】
日本の通貨は円。紙幣は1,000、2,000、5,000、1万円の4種類、硬貨は1、5、10、50、100、500円の6種類ある。1$=約93円、1ユーロ=約113円、1豪ドル=約79円（2010年6月現在）。

【電圧】
100ボルト、50/60ヘルツ。家庭製品をそのまま使う場合は、変圧器とアダプターが必要になることもある。コンセントの形状はAタイプ。

【郵便】
切手は郵便局やコンビニで購入できる。海外へのハガキは70円、封書は送り先と重さで異なる。投函は街中の赤いポストへ。

Temperature Comparison 温度比較

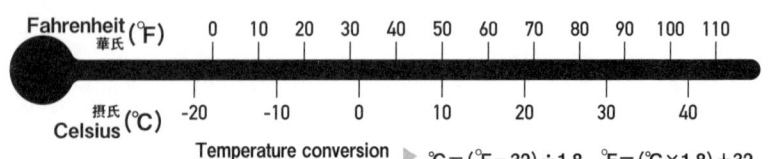

Fahrenheit (°F): 0 10 20 30 40 50 60 70 80 90 100 110
Celsius (°C): -20 -10 0 10 20 30 40

Temperature conversion 温度表示の算出の仕方 ▶ °C = (°F − 32) ÷ 1.8   °F = (°C × 1.8) + 32

Weights and Measures 度量衡

Length 長さ

Metric メートル法

Meter メートル	Kilometer キロ
1	0.001
1000	1
0.025	-
0.305	-
0.914	0.0009
1609	1.609
0.030	-
0.303	0.0003
1.818	0.002

U.S./Imperial system ヤード・ポンド法

Inch インチ	Foot/feet フィート	Yard ヤード	Mile マイル
39.370	3.281	1.094	-
39370	3281	1094.1	0.621
1	0.083	0.028	-
12.00	1	0.333	-
36.00	3.00	1	0.0006
63360	5280	1760	1
1.193	0.099	0.033	-
11.930	0.994	0.331	0.0002
71.583	5.965	1.988	0.001

Old Japanese system 尺貫法

Kairi 海里	Sun 寸	Shaku 尺	Ken 間
-	33.00	3.300	0.550
0.540	33000	3300	550.0
-	0.838	0.084	0.014
-	10.058	1.006	0.168
0.0004	30.175	3.017	0.503
0.869	53107	5310.7	885.12
-	1	0.100	0.017
0.0002	10.00	1	0.167
0.0009	60.00	6.00	1

Weight 重さ

U.S./Metric メートル法

Gram グラム	Kilogram キログラム	Ton トン
1	0.001	-
1000	1	0.001
-	1000	1
28.349	0.028	0.00003
453.59	0.453	0.0005
3.750	0.004	-
3750	3.750	0.004
600.0	0.600	0.0006

U.S./Imperial system ヤード・ポンド法

Ounce オンス	Pound ポンド
0.035	0.002
35.274	2.205
35274	2204.6
1	0.0625
16.00	1
0.132	0.008
132.2	8.267
21.164	1.322

Old Japanese system 尺貫法

Monme 匁	Kan 貫	Kin 斤
0.267	0.0003	0.002
266.667	0.267	1.667
266667	266.667	1666.67
7.560	0.008	0.047
120.958	0.121	0.756
1	0.001	0.006
1000	1	6.250
160.0	0.160	1

Area 面積

Metric メートル法

Are (100 sq meters) アール	Square kilometer 平方キロメートル
1	0.0001
10000	1
40.469	0.004
25906	2.59067
0.033	0.000003
9.917	0.00099
99.174	0.0099

U.S./Imperial system ヤード・ポンド法

Acre エーカー	Square mile 平方マイル
0.025	0.00004
247.11	0.386
1	0.0016
640.0	1
0.0008	-
0.245	0.0004
2.450	0.004

Old Japanese system 尺貫法

Tsubo 坪	Tan 反	Cho 町
30.250	0.100	0.010
302500	1008.3	100.83
1224.12	4.080	0.408
783443	2611.42	261.14
1	0.003	0.0003
300.0	1	0.100
3000.0	10.000	1

Volume 体積

Metric メートル法

Cubic centimeter 立方センチ	Liter リットル	Cubic meter 立方メートル
1	0.001	0.000001
1000	1	0.001
-	1000	1
946.35	0.946	0.0009
3785.4	3.785	0.004
180.39	0.180	0.00018
1803.9	1.804	0.0018
18039	18.04	0.018

U.S./Imperial system ヤード・ポンド法

Quart クォート	U.S. gallon 米ガロン
0.0011	0.0002
1.057	0.264
1056.8	264.19
1	0.25
4.00	1
0.191	0.048
1.906	0.476
19.060	4.766

Old Japanese system 尺貫法

Go 合	Sho 升	To 斗
0.006	0.0006	0.00006
5.543	0.554	0.055
5543.5	554.35	55.435
5.246	0.525	0.052
20.983	2.098	0.210
1	0.100	0.010
10.00	1	0.100
100.00	10.00	1

Learn more about Japan
日本にまつわる雑学ガイド

1. Japan's notoriously crowded trains
悪名高い日本の満員電車

Japan's crowded trains are world-famous. In large cities it's not unusual to see station attendants pushing people onto trains, which are so crowded that some people even end up with broken ribs. Some say it's actually easier to ride on trains that are so packed that you don't have to stand up on your own.

Recently more people commute at staggered times to avoid the rush hour, or commute by bicycle. Some railways encourage staggered commute by offering benefits to early-morning users. There are also trains with seats that can be folded up during rush hour to make room for more passengers.

Groping is also prevalent on crowded trains. Due to some highly-publicized cases of men being falsely accused of groping, many men are careful to avoid being mistaken for a groper (e.g., by keeping both hands on the straps). Some railways have addressed this problem by providing "women only" cars in the morning and/or late at night, usually identifiable by pink stickers. (These cars can also be used by children and disabled men.) Men, be careful not to get on these cars!

今や世界的に有名な日本の満員電車。大都市では、なかなか電車に乗り込めない乗客を駅員がぎゅうぎゅう押し込む風景も珍しくなく、押されて肋骨を骨折した人もいるほどだ。一方、すし詰めの満員電車では自分で立っていなくてもいいので逆に楽、という意見も。

最近は、ラッシュアワーを避けてフレックスタイムで時差通勤したり、自転車通勤したりする人が増えてきた。電車の早朝利用に特典を用意するなど、時差通勤のキャンペーンを実施する鉄道会社も出てきた。また、ラッシュ時には座席を折りたたんで、より多くの客が乗車できるようになっている車両もある。

混雑する電車では、痴漢も多発する。痴漢と間違えられて冤罪となった事件が問題になったこともあり、男性は両手で吊り革につかまるなどして、痴漢に間違えられないように気をつけている人が多いという。さらに、痴漢対策として、朝や深夜に女性専用車両（子供や体の不自由な人などは男性でも乗車可）が設けられている路線もある。通常ピンク系のステッカーが目印になっている。男性は間違えて乗り込まないように御注意を。

2. Strange English is everywhere!
街には変な英語が大氾濫！

In Japan you see many T-shirts, bags, etc. with strange English on them. This is because the English is written by Japanese people without much thought for accuracy. It's not just spelling mistakes: you'll find expressions ("So much special！") that make some sense but are slightly off, as well as expressions that are grammatically correct but make no sense at all. Outside of Japan, on the other hand, you'll occasionally see people wearing T-shirts with strange Japanese. And Britney Spears has a tattoo that says "変" (strange). (Apparently she wanted a tattoo meaning "mysterious.")

日本では変な英語の書いてあるTシャツやバッグなどが多い。日本人が適当に考えて書いているために変な英語になってしまうのだ。スペルの間違いなどはもちろんのこと、"So much special！"のように意味はなんとなくわかるものの間違った英語、また文法的には合っていても意味不明な英語などさまざまだ。一方外国では変な日本語の書かれたTシャツを着ている人を見かける。ブリトニー・スピアーズは「変」というタトゥーをしているし…(本人は"mysterious"という意味で注文したようだ)。

3. Young people dependent on their parents
親に依存して生きる若者たち

Young people who do not find employment and continue to live with their parents after graduation are called "parasite singles." Job scarcity and changing family relations are partly to blame for this phenomenon; but Japan has never been a place where children are strongly encouraged to live on their own.

In 2000, the number of adults living with their parents rose to 12 million, and this is one cause of the high ratio of unmarried people and low birth rate. South Korea and Western countries are also experiencing similar problems.

高校や大学卒業後、職にも就かず結婚もせずに親と同居し、日常生活の面倒を見てもらう若者を「パラサイトシングル」と呼ぶ。背景には親子関係の変化や就職難などが考えられるが、日本ではもともと子供は早く親から独立して生活すべきという考え方が強くないということもある。

親と同居している成人の数は、2000年には1200万人にも上り、これは日本の未婚率の高さや少子化などの一因となっている。「パラサイトシングル」と似た状況は、欧米や韓国などでも問題になっている。

4. "Japlish" is Japanese
「和製英語」も日本語の一部

"Order made," "jet coaster," "energish," etc...There are countless "Japlish" expressions that are only understood in Japan. Some Japanese actually think these are English expressions and will try to say these with an "English-like" accent when talking to foreigners.

Some of these expressions have a different meaning in Japanese. For example, "smart (*sumaato*)" means "slim (figure)," rather than "clever"; and "mansion (*manshon*)" is used to refer to an ordinary high-rise dwelling. Such expressions may be a "misuse of English"; but they are firmly entrenched in the Japanese language.

「オーダーメイド」「ジェットコースター」「エネルギッシュ」「イメージダウン」などなど…。日本でしか通じない和製英語は数え切れない。英語だと思っていて、英語っぽく発音すれば通じると思っている日本人もいる。

また本来の英語とは違った意味で使われるものもある。たとえば、本来「賢い」の意味となる「smart→スマート」が「スリムな体型」を表したり、「豪邸」を表す「mansion→マンション」が普通の高層集合住宅を表したりも。こうした造語は「英語の誤用」かもしれないが、日本語として定着しているのである。

5. Fatally hard-working: "karōshi"
勤勉さが命取り——深刻な「過労死」

Death from stroke, heart attack or other illness brought on by extreme working conditions is called "*karōshi*," or "death from overwork." It also refers to suicides caused by overwork-induced depression.

Awareness of overwork has been rising and counseling has become more widely available; but since a cause-effect relationship is hard to establish, only 10% of cases are recognized as work-related deaths.

"*Karōshi*" is a Japanese phenomenon, and tends to increase in times of recession as anxiety about unemployment results in "over-adaptation."

長時間労働や休日なしの過度の労働のため、脳溢血や心臓麻痺などで死亡することを「過労死」という。また、過酷な状況のせいでうつ病になり、自殺する場合も含めて言う。

最近では過労に対する意識が高まり、相談センターも増えてきた。しかし、因果関係を特定するのが難しいので、労働災害として認定されるのは1割程度に過ぎない。

「過労死」は日本独自の現象と言われ、不況期には、失業への不安から長時間労働に過剰適応し、増加する傾向にある。

6. Japan, land of "cosplay"
コスプレ王国日本

Large-scale "costume play" events are frequently held at stadiums, and it is now widely known that you can find many "cosplay" fans in Harajuku and in the "maid cafés" of Akihabara, Tokyo.

Cosplay is often thought of as a hobby limited to a small group of enthusiasts, but Japanese people's love of cosplay is a widespread phenomenon. In Kyoto, people walk around dressed up as maiko; the samurai and ninja cosplay attraction at Toei's Studio Park is extremely popular; and Halloween events at Disneyland are nothing less than cosplay rallies for adults and children alike.

日本では球場などで大規模なコスプレイベントが頻繁に開催され、東京の秋葉原のメイドカフェや原宿などでもコスプレを楽しむ人に多く出会えるのは、もはや周知の通り。

「コスプレ」と言うと一部のマニアだけといっイメージもあるが、日本人のコスプレ好きは一般に広がっている。京都では舞妓さんに扮して街を歩き写真撮影する「舞妓体験」や、太秦映画村での武士や忍者コスプレが大人気だし、ディズニーランドをはじめとするハロウィーンイベントなども、大人も子供も一緒に楽しむコスプレ大会と化している。

7. "Herbivore men" and "carnivore women"
草食系男子 VS 肉食系女子

Young men who do not take the initiative in romantic relationships and are not "hungry" for the opposite sex are called "herbivore men." Rather than pursuing romantic relationships, they are more interested in being friends with women, place importance on family, and do household chores traditionally associated with women. They are sensitive, unambitious, and prefer to avoid confrontation. In one survey, 75% of men in their 20s and 30s identified themselves as "Herbivore men." Correspondingly, women who are assertive in matters of love and sex have come to be called "carnivore women."

恋愛やセックスに積極的でなく、異性に対してガツガツしない20〜30代の男性を「草食系男子」という。恋愛よりも、女性との友達づきあいや家族を大切にし、女性がやるべきと考えられてきた家事などもこなす。また性格は繊細で、出世欲は強くなく、争いを好まないのが特徴。ある調査では、自分を「草食系男子」と考える20〜30代の男性は75％という数字も出ている。こうした男性が増えるなか、恋愛やセックスに積極的な女性を指す「肉食系女子」という言葉も登場した。

8. Want to get married? Do "*konkatsu*"!
婚活なしには結婚できない?!

"*Shūshoku katsudō*" (job hunting) is called "*shūkatsu*"; but more and more young people are busy with "*konkatsu*" ("*kekkon katsudō*," or "spouse hunting"). Whereas before women would often quit their jobs after getting married, the Equal Opportunity Law and changing values and economic conditions have made it harder for people to find romance in their daily lives.

Specifically, "*konkatsu*" includes everything from marriage counseling and dating parties, to men taking cake making lessons to meet women and re-examining their marriage partner criteria.

「就職活動」を略して「就活」というが、就活ならぬ「婚活（結婚活動の略）」にいそしむ20～30代の男女が増えている。かつては会社を寿退社する女性社員も多かったが、男女雇用機会均等法の制定や経済状況・価値観の変化で、自然な恋愛結婚が難しくなってきたことが理由に考えられる。

具体的には、結婚相談所の利用やお見合いパーティーに参加することを始めとして、男性がケーキ教室に参加するなど出会いの場を求めて習い事を始める、相手に要求する条件を見直す、といったことも「婚活」に含まれる。

9. Pets: part of the family
ペットも大切な家族の一員

With the recent popularity of pets, there has been an increase in dog-friendly "dog cafés." Some of these places offer dishes that are not at all inferior to human fare. And now there are also "cat cafés," where customers can frolic with cats.

More and more apartments allow residents to keep pets, and on major travel sites you can do searches of "pet-friendly accommodations." More people are willing to spend money on their pets, too, as witnessed by the rise in popularity of upscale pet clothing, pet insurance, and Buddhist pet funerals and cremations.

近年のペットブームで、犬を同伴できる「ドッグカフェ」が増えている。なかには、人間の食事に引けを取らないペット用のメニューを用意している店もある。さらに、猫と戯れる空間を提供する「猫カフェ」も登場した。

ペットを飼えるマンションも増えてきたし、主要な旅行サイトでは「ペットと泊まれる宿」が検索できるようになっている。ペットにお金をかける人も増え、高級ブランド衣類などはもとより、保険に加入させたり、寺院で葬儀をして納骨する人も増えてきた。

10. Giving children a head start
子どもには英語で苦労させたくないから…

Surveys on lessons taken by small children show that the most popular subject, beating out swimming and piano, is English. Apparently, the idea that children should be given a head start in English is no longer a minority view. Even ordinary kindergartens have started to incorporate English into their curriculum. Expensive English textbook sets and English preschools (that cost more than twice as much as general private kindergartens) are also popular.

English will soon be compulsory from the 5th grade. Will Japanese people's English conversation ability improve?

幼児の習い事ランキングではスイミングやピアノを押さえて英語教室がNo.1となり、「幼児のうちから英語を始めるべき」はもはや常識となっている。普通の幼稚園でも、英会話の時間を取り入れるところも出てきた。さらには、英語教室だけでなく、高額なセット教材や、一般的な私立幼稚園の2倍以上の費用がかかる英語プリスクールも大人気。

小学校5年生からの英語必修化も決定した。この先日本人の英会話力は向上することになるのだろうか?

11. Japan's costly funerals
お金のかかる日本のお葬式

Many people in Japan have Christian-style weddings regardless of their actual religious beliefs, but funerals are mostly conducted in the Buddhist style. Japanese funerals are quite costly in comparison to other developed countries: the average funeral costs roughly 2.3 million yen. 1.4 million of this goes to the funeral company, 400,000 is for food/drink served to guests, and 500,000 is for donations to the temple and "tips" to people helping out.

Nowadays more people are opting for less costly alternatives such as cremation-only "*chokusō*."

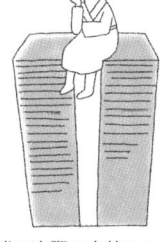

日本では、結婚式は実際の宗教にかかわらずキリスト教式で挙げる人が多いが、葬儀は仏式で執り行う人が多い。日本の葬儀の平均費用は約230万円と、先進諸外国と比べてかなり高めになっている。内訳は、葬儀会社に払う葬儀一式の費用が140万円、飲食接待費用が40万円、お寺へのお布施、お手伝いの方への心付けが50万程度となっている。

一方、葬儀をせず火葬する「直葬」を行うなど、費用をかけないケースも増えている。

Sound more natural in Japanese! 会話が広がる！

Useful expressions
簡単ひとことフレーズ講座

Japanese conversations are sprinkled with onomatopoeic and mimetic words that convey feelings or describe movement accurately and directly. Here are some useful, uniquely Japanese expressions and their examples.

会話の中にしばしば登場する擬態語、擬音語は、相手の感情や動きを、より的確に、よりストレートに伝えてくれる。ここでは知っておくと便利な、日本語独特の表現とその例文をまとめて紹介しよう。

■Sound Effects 擬態語・擬音語

[グズグズ / guzuguzu]

グズグズしていて遅刻する
guzuguzu shiteite chikoku suru
to be late after dilly-dallying
トゥ ビ レイト アフタァ ディリィダリィング

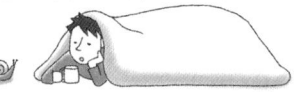

The state of dawdling and/or being slow to take action. Also means to "complain," to become "loose," or a state of being "unclear/unsettled" (as in "〜 weather").

敏速に行動せずのろのろしている様子を表す。また「〜した態度」「〜になる」「〜した天気」のように不平不満を言うさま、ゆるんだり、はっきりしないさまを表すのにも使われる。

[ムカムカ / mukamuka]

あいつにはムカムカする
aitsu ni wa mukamuka suru
He really pisses me off.
ヒ リアリィ ピスィズ ミ オフ

Feeling of repugnance or pent-up anger. Same as "mukatto." Also used to describe a state of nausea, as in "i ga mukamuka suru" ("I feel sick to my stomach").

極度の嫌悪や、やり場のない怒りが込み上げるさまを表す。「ムカっと」も同様の意味で使われる。また、「胃がムカムカする」のように気持ちが悪く吐きそうな様子を表す。

[ブラブラ / burabura]

家でブラブラしている
ie de burabura shiteiru
hang out at home
ハング アウト アット ホウム

The state of "dangling," or leading an idle life. Also used to describe the state of walking around in a leisurely, aimless manner, as in "kōen o 〜 sampo suru" (" 〜 walk in the park").

ぶら下がって揺れているさまや、仕事にも就かずに怠惰な生活をする様子を表す。また、「公園を〜散歩する」のように、のんびりと歩いて回ったりするさまを表すのにも使われる。

[もっさり / mossari]

もっさりした服装
mossari shita fukusoo
unfashionable clothes
アンファッショナブゥ クロウズ

Used to describe someone who looks unfashionable and unsophisticated, or someone who is sluggish and slow to respond. Also means "bushy," as in "bushy hair."

外見や服装が野暮ったくて垢抜けていない様子や、動作や反応が遅くて気が利かないことを表す。また、「〜した髪」などのように、髪や毛が多くて野暮ったいさまを表すときにも使われる。

知っておこう

まったり
mattari

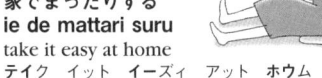

家でまったりする
ie de mattari suru
take it easy at home
テイク イット イーズィ アット ホウム

In addition to describing a mellow, full-bodied taste, it has recently come to mean "taking it easy" or "lack of motivation."

「～した味」など、まろやかでコクのある味わいを表すほか、近年ではのんびりと過ごす様子や、やる気のない様子を表すのにも使われるようになった。

ペコペコ
pekopeko

ペコペコお辞儀をする
pekopeko ojigi o suru
bow repeatedly (in a servile manner)
バウ リピーティドリィ (イン ア サーァヴゥ マナァ)

The state of kowtowing to someone, or the state/sound of being hollowed, as in "*onaka ga pekopeko da* (I'm starving)."

やたらと下手に出て、相手にこびへつらい機嫌を取る態度を表すほか、「お腹が～だ」など、へこんだ様子や音を表す。

ピリピリ
piripiri

ピリピリした雰囲気
piripiri shita fun-iki
a tense atmosphere
ア テンス アトモスフィアァ

A state of tension or oversensitivity. Also used to describe a burning sensation, as in "～ *shita karasa*" ("a burning spiciness"), or the sound of thin paper tearing.

緊張や過敏な神経を表す。また「～した辛さ」など刺すような感覚、薄紙を破る音を表す。

メロメロ
meromero

孫にメロメロになる
mago ni meromero ni naru
has a soft spot for his grandson
ハズ ア ソフト スパット フォア ヒズ グランドサン

The state of being so infatuated with a person or pet that you can't control yourself and don't care what other people think.

自制心や抵抗力を失って、人の目も気にせずに、蕩けるほど異性やペットなどに夢中になる様子を表すのに使われる。

コツコツ
kotsukotsu

コツコツ貯金する
kotsukotsu chokin suru
steadily save up money
ステディリィ セイヴ アップ マニィ

The state of working steadily at something, little by little. Also an onomatopoeic word for the clacking sound of something hard, such as high heels.

地道な努力を少しずつ続ける様子を表す。ハイヒールの足音など、硬いものが触れ合うときの音を表す。

がっつり
gattsuri

がっつり食べる
gattsuri taberu
eat to your heart's content
イート トゥ ユアァ ハーァツ コンテント

An expression meaning "thoroughly," "plentifully," "to your heart's content." Thought by some to be a Hokkaido expression that came into general use.

「しっかり」「たっぷり」「思う存分」という意味を表す。北海道の方言が全国的に広まったとも言われている。

Vocabulary list
American English ➡ Japanese
アメリカ英語 ➡ 日本語
アルファベット順日本語単語帳

A

accept	受け取る / uketoru
accident report	事故証明書 / jiko shoomei sho
ache	痛む / itamu
actually	実は / jitsuwa
additional charge	追加料金 / tsuika ryookin
address	住所 / juusho
adjust	調節する / choosetsu suru
adult	成人 / seijin
advance ticket	前売券 / maeuri ken
agree	賛成する / sansei suru
air conditioning	冷房 / reiboo
airport	空港 / kuukoo
aisle	通路 / tsuuro
all-day pass	1日券 / ichinichi ken
allergy	アレルギー / arerugii
ambulance	救急車 / kyuukyuusha
anemia	貧血 / hinketsu
anniversary	記念日 / kinenbi
appetite	食欲 / shokuyoku
application form	申込用紙 / mooshikomi yooshi
apply for ~	~に申込む / ~ ni mooshikomu
appreciate	感謝する / kansha suru
area	地域 / chiiki
arrange	手配する / tehai suru
arrive	到着する / toochaku suru
ashtray	灰皿 / haizara
ask	尋ねる / tazuneru
aspirin	アスピリン / asupirin
asthma	ぜんそく / zensoku
attractive	魅力的な / miryokuteki na

B

backache	腰痛 / yootsuu
baggage	荷物 / nimotsu
bank account	銀行口座 / ginkoo kooza
bathroom (for bathing)	浴室 / yokushitsu
battery	電池 / denchi
be late	遅刻 / chikoku
beautiful	美しい / utsukushii
bedroom	寝室 / shinshitsu
before tax	税抜きで / zeinuki de
begin	始まる / hajimaru
beginner	初心者 / shoshinsha
behind	後ろ / ushiro
bills, paper money	紙幣 / shihei
blanket	毛布 / moofu
bleed	出血する / shukketsu suru
blood pressure	血圧 / ketsuatsu
blood type	血液型 / ketsueki gata
body temperature	体温 / taion
bone fracture	骨折 / kossetsu
boring	退屈な / taikutsu na
borrow	借りる / kariru
break	壊れる / kowareru
break down, fail	故障する / koshoo suru
breakfast	朝食 / chooshoku
breathe	呼吸する / kokyuu suru
bright	明るい / akarui
brochure	パンフレット / panfuretto
bruise	打撲 / daboku
budget	予算 / yosan
building	ビル／建物 / biru/tatemono
bully	いじめる / ijimeru
burn	やけど / yakedo
business hours	営業時間 / eigyoo jikan
buy	買う / kau
by bus	バスで / basu de
by plane	飛行機で / hikooki de
by train	電車で / densha de

C

calculate	計算する	keisan suru
call out to, summon	呼ぶ	yobu
cancel	キャンセルする	kyanseru suru
car rental	レンタカー	rentakaa
carry	運ぶ	hakobu
cash	現金	genkin
cashier	レジ	reji
change (from a purchase)	お釣り	otsuri
change trains, buses, etc.	乗り換える	norikaeru
change, revise	変更する	henkoo suru
charge a customer for a purchase	請求する	seikyuu suru
charming	魅力的な	miryokuteki na
cheap	安い	yasui
check (one's baggage)	預ける	azukeru
check, bill	勘定	kanjoo
cheerful	明るい	akarui
cherry blossoms	桜	sakura
children	子供	kodomo
choose	選ぶ	erabu
chopsticks	箸	hashi
chronic	慢性の	mansei no
cigarettes	たばこ	tabako
clean	掃除する	sooji suru
clock	時計	tokei
close	閉める／閉じる	shimeru/tojiru
cloudy	曇りの	kumori no
coins	硬貨	kooka
cold (weather)	寒い	samui
cold medicine	風邪薬	kazegusuri
cold, chilled	冷たい	tsumetai
collect call	コレクトコール	korekuto kooru
come	来る	kuru
come back	戻る	modoru
comfortable, enjoyable	快適な	kaiteki na
complaint	クレーム	kureemu
confirm	確認する	kakunin suru
(be) congested (with traffic)	渋滞している	juutai shiteiru
constipation	便秘	bempi
consult	相談する	soodan suru
consumption tax	消費税	shoohizei
contact	連絡する	renraku suru
contact information	連絡先	renraku saki
contact lens solution	コンタクト洗浄液	kontakuto senjoo eki
continue	続ける	tsuzukeru
cool, refreshing	涼しい	suzushii
corner	角	kado
correct	正しい	tadashii
cosmetics	化粧品	keshoohin
cough	咳	seki
count	数える	kazoeru
courier service	宅配便	takuhaibin
crosswalk	横断歩道	oodan hodoo
(be) crowded	混雑している	konzatsu shiteiru
cry	泣く	naku
custom	習慣	shuukan
cute	かわいい	kawaii

D

dangerous	危ない	abunai
dark	暗い	kurai
dead end	行き止まり	ikidomari
deceive	だます	damasu
decline	断る	kotowaru
delicious	おいしい	oishii
deliver	届ける	todokeru
dentist	歯医者	haisha
deposit	前金	maekin
destination	目的地	mokutekichi
diabetes	糖尿病	toonyoo byoo
diarrhea	下痢	geri
different	違う	chigau
digital camera	デジカメ	dejikame
dinner	夕食	yuushoku
dip	少し浸す	sukoshi hitasu
dirty	汚れた	yogoreta
discount	割引	waribiki
disinfectant	消毒液	shoodoku eki
distance	距離	kyori
dizziness	めまい	memai
doctor	医者	isha

137

dotted line	点線 tensen	evening	夕方 yuugata	food	食べ物 tabemono
doubt	疑う utagau	exchange	交換する kookan suru	food poisoning	食あたり shokuatari
drink	飲み物 nomimono	exit	出口 deguchi	forbid	禁止する kinshi suru
drive	運転する unten suru	expensive	高い takai	forget	忘れる wasureru
drop	落とす otosu	explode	爆発する bakuhatsu suru	fragile	壊れ物 kowaremono
drop off (rental cars)	乗り捨てる norisuteru	expressway	高速道路 koosoku dooro	fraud	詐欺 sagi
drunk	酔った yotta	eye drops	目薬 megusuri	free	無料の muryoo no
dry cleaning	クリーニング kuriiningu	**F**		friend	友だち tomodachi
duty-free shop	免税店 menzeiten	facility	設備 setsubi	front desk	フロント furonto
E		faint, pass out	意識をなくす ishiki o nakusu	full (of people)	満席の manseki no
early	早い hayai	famous	有名な yuumei na	funny	おもしろい omoshiroi
eat	食べる taberu	far	遠い tooi	**G**	
eat out	外食する gaishoku suru	fashionable	流行の ryuukoo no	garden	庭 niwa
effect	効果 kooka	fast	速い hayai	gas station	ガソリンスタンド gasorin sutando
electric light	電気 denki	fee	手数料／料金 tesuuryoo/ryookin	(medical) gauze	ガーゼ gaaze
electrical outlet	コンセント konsento	feel sick	気分が悪い kibun ga warui	get better, heal	治る naoru
embarrassed	恥ずかしい hazukashii	(have a) fever	熱がある netsu ga aru	get changed	着替える kigaeru
embassy	大使館 taishikan	few	少ない sukunai	get hurt	ケガをする kega o suru
emergency	緊急の kinkyuu no	find	見つける mitsukeru	get lost	道に迷う michi ni mayoo
emergency exit	非常口 hijooguchi	finish	終わる／終える owaru/oeru	get off	降りる oriru
emergency line	110番／119番 hyaku too ban/ hyaku juu kyuu ban	fire	火事 kaji	give	あげる ageru
emergency measure	応急処置 ookyuu shochi	fire station	消防署 shooboo sho	glad	うれしい ureshii
energetic, lively	元気な genki na	fit well	ピッタリ合う pittari au	glasses	眼鏡 megane
enjoy	楽しむ tanoshimu	fitting room	試着室 shichaku shitsu	go	行く iku
entrance	入口 iriguchi	fix	直す naosu	go across	渡る wataru
entrance fee	入場料 nyuujooryoo	flashy	派手な hade na	go back	戻る modoru
		fly	飛ぶ tobu	go out	外出する gaishutsu suru

go straight	直進する chokushin suru				
grab	つかむ tsukamu				

H / I / J

		immediately	すぐに suguni	Japanese-style room	和室 washitsu
half-day	半日の han-nichi no	important	重要な juuyoo na	jet lag	時差ボケ jisaboke
hand over	渡す watasu	in time	間に合って maniatte		
hang	掛ける kakeru	indigestion	消化不良 shookafuryoo	key	鍵 kagi
hangover	二日酔い futsukayoi	infant	幼児 yooji	know	知る shiru
happen	起こる okoru	information	情報 joohoo		
happy	幸せな shiawase na	ingredient	材料 zairyoo	lake	湖 mizuumi
hard, solid	硬い katai	injection	注射 chuusha	laptop computer	ノートパソコン nooto pasokon
hate	嫌いだ kirai da	insect repellent	虫除け mushiyoke	large	大きい ookii
have a cold	風邪 kaze	inspection	検査 kensa	last name	名字 myooji
heater	暖房 danboo	instead of 〜	〜の代わりに 〜 no kawari ni	last train	最終電車 saishuu densha
heatstroke	熱中症 necchuushoo	insult	侮辱する bujoku suru	(be) late	遅れる okureru
heavy	重い omoi	insurance	保険 hoken	late at night	深夜に shin-ya ni
high	高い takai	interesting	おもしろい omoshiroi	later	あとで ato de
high blood pressure	高血圧 kooketsuatsu	internal medicine	内科 naika	latest	最新の saishin no
hobby	趣味 shumi	international call	国際電話 kokusai denwa	laundry	洗濯 sentaku
honeymoon	新婚旅行 shinkon ryokoo	international driver's license	国際運転免許証 kokusai unten menkyo shoo	leave	出る deru
hospital	病院 byooin	Internet access	ネット接続 netto setsuzoku	lend	貸す kasu
hot (to the touch)	熱い atsui	interpreter	通訳 tsuuyaku	lie down	横になる yoko ni naru
hot (weather)	暑い atsui	intersection	交差点 koosaten	lighter	ライター raitaa
hot water	お湯 oyu	intravenous drip	点滴 tenteki	lightweight	軽い karui
humid	ジメジメした jimejime shita	introduce	紹介する shookai suru	like	好きだ suki da
humidity	湿度 shitsudo	invite	招待する shootai suru	live	住む sumu
(be) hungry	お腹が空いた onaka ga suita	(be) irritated	イライラする iraira suru	local train	各駅停車 kakueki teisha
hurry	急ぐ isogu	issue, publish	発行する hakkoo suru	locker (coin-operated)	コインロッカー koin rokkaa

long	長い nagai	menstrual period	生理 seiri	nonsmoking section	禁煙席 kin-enseki
look	見る miru	message	伝言 dengon	nonstop	直行便 chokkoobin
look after ~	~の世話をする ~ no sewa o suru	meticulous	几帳面な kichoomen na	noon	昼／正午 hiru/shoogo
look for ~	~を探す ~ o sagasu	midnight	深夜 shin-ya	notice	気づく kizuku
look like ~	~に似ている ~ ni niteiru	mirror	鏡 kagami	number	番号 bangoo
loose	ゆるい yurui	miss (a train, etc.)	乗り損なう norisokonau	nurse	看護士 kangoshi
lose (something)	なくす nakusu	missing, lost	紛失した funshitsu shita	**O**	
lose one's way	迷子になる maigo ni naru	mobile phone	携帯電話 keitai denwa	observation point	展望台 temboodai
lost and found	遺失物相談所 ishitsubutsu soodanjo	money	お金 okane	occupied	使用中 shiyoochuu
loud	大きい声で ookii koe de	morning	朝 asa	office	事務所 jimusho
low	低い hikui	motion sickness	乗り物酔い norimono yoi	okay	大丈夫 daijoobu
low blood pressure	低血圧 teiketsuatsu	motion sickness bag	エチケット袋 echiketto bukuro	old	古い furui
lunch	昼食 chuushoku	mouthwash (antiseptic)	うがい薬 ugai gusuri	on foot	徒歩で toho de
M		**N**		on the way	途中で tochuu de
make a mistake	間違う machigau	narrow	狭い semai	on time	定刻 teikoku
make a reservation	予約する yoyaku suru	narrow	細い hosoi	one-day	日帰りの higaeri no
many	多い ooi	(be) nauseous	吐き気がする hakike ga suru	open	開ける akeru
map	地図 chizu	near	近い chikai	operation	手術 shujutsu
married couple	夫婦 fuufu	necessary	必要な hitsuyoo na	optometry	眼科 ganka
meal	食事 shokuji	negotiate	交渉する kooshoo suru	other	ほかの hoka no
medical certificate	診断書 shindansho	neighborhood	近所 kinjo	(on the) other side	反対側の hantai gawa no
medical examination	診察 shinsatsu	new	新しい atarashii	otolaryngology	耳鼻咽喉科 jibi inkoo ka
medical specialist	専門医 semmon-i	next	次の tsugi no	out of order	故障して koshoo shite
medicine	薬 kusuri	night	夜 yoru	outside	外で soto de
meet	会う au	no parking	駐車禁止 chuusha kinshi	**P**	
menstrual cramps	生理痛 seiritsuu	noise	騒音 soo-on	pain	痛み itami
		non-reserved seat	自由席 jiyuu seki	painkiller	鎮痛剤 chintsuuzai

English	Japanese	Romaji
parking lot	駐車場	chuushajoo
pass	渡す	watasu
passenger	乗客	jyookyaku
passing through	通過	tsuuka
pay	支払う	shiharau
pay a bill	精算する	seisan suru
pay in advance	先払いする	sakibarai suru
pedestrian overpass	横断歩道橋	oodan hodookyoo
pediatrics	小児科	shooni ka
personal computer	パソコン	pasokon
pharmacy	薬局	yakkyoku
pick up, gather	拾う	hirou
pickpocket	すり	suri
picky	好き嫌いが多い	sukikirai ga ooi
pill	錠剤	joozai
place	場所	basho
plane ticket	航空券	kookuuken
platform	ホーム	hoomu
pneumonia	肺炎	haien
police car	パトカー	patokaa
police officer	警察官	keisatsukan
politics	政治	ooiji
post office	郵便局	yuubinkyoku
postal code	郵便番号	yuubin bangoo
postage	郵便料金	yuubin ryookin
postcard	ハガキ	hagaki
power source	電源	dengen
pregnant	妊娠中	ninshin chuu
prescription	処方箋	shohoosen
price	値段／価格	nedan/kakaku
private room	個室	koshitsu
problem	問題	mondai
protest	反対する	hantai suru
public restroom	公衆トイレ	kooshuu toire
public transportation	交通機関	kootsuu kikan
pull	引く	hiku
pulse	脈拍	myakuhaku
purpose	目的	mokuteki
purse-snatcher	ひったくり	hittakuri
push	押す	osu

Q

quiet	静かな	shizuka na

R

railway crossing	踏み切り	fumikiri
rain	雨	ame
raise	上げる	ageru
razor	カミソリ	kamisori
(be) ready	準備ができた	jumbi ga dekita
reason	理由	riyuu
receive	受け取る	uketoru
recharge	充電	juuden
record	記録／記録する	kiroku/kiroku suru
refund	返金する／払戻し	henkin suru/haraimodoshi
register	登録する	tooroku suru
reissue	再発行する	saihakkoo suru
relax	のんびりする／くつろぐ	nombiri suru/kutsurogu
relaxed (atmosphere)	落ち着いた	ochitsuita
repeat	繰り返す	kurikaesu
report	報告する	hookoku suru
reserved seat	指定席	shitei seki
rest area	休憩場所	kyuukei basho
restroom	トイレ	toire
return	返す	kaesu
ride (a bus, train, etc.)	乗る	noru
right	右	migi
robber, robbery	強盗	gootoo
route	順路	junro
route map	路線図	rosenzu

S

English	Japanese	Romaji
safe	安全な	anzen na
safe, vault	金庫	kinko
sanitary products	生理用品	seiri yoohin
(be) satisfied	満足だ	manzoku da
scary	怖い	kowai
scenic	眺めのいい	nagame no ii
seat	席	seki
sell	売る	uru
send	送る	okuru
separate	別々の	betsubetsu no
service charge	サービス料	saabisu ryoo

141

shake hands	握手する akushu suru	souvenir	みやげ miyage	sunset	日没 nichibotsu
share	シェアする shea suru	spicy	辛い karai	suntan lotion	日焼け止め hiyake dome
ship	船 fune	split the bill	割り勘にする warikan ni suru	surgery	外科／手術 geka/shujutsu
short (in height)	低い hikui	sprain	ねんざ nenza	surname	名字 myooji
short (in length)	短い mijikai	stairs	階段 kaidan	(be) surprised	驚いた odoroita
shoulder	肩 kata	stand, newsstand	売店 baiten	sweet	甘い amai
show	見せる miseru	state, province	州 shuu	symptom	症状 shoojoo
sick	病気の byooki no	station	駅 eki	**T**	
side effect	副作用 fukusayoo	stay	滞在する taizai suru	table (at a restaurant)	椅子席 isu seki
sidewalk	歩道 hodoo	stomach	胃 i	take a picture	写真をとる shashin o toru
sign	署名する shomei suru	stomach medicine	胃腸薬 ichooyaku	take along	持っていく motteiku
signal light	信号 shingoo	stomachache	腹痛 fukutsuu	take one's measurements	採寸する saisun suru
signature	署名 shomei	stop the bleeding	止血する shiketsu suru	talk	話す hanasu
signboard	看板 kamban	straight ahead	前方の zempoo no	tall	高い takai
sit	座る suwaru	strange	変な／奇妙な hen na/kimyoo na	taste bad	まずい mazui
situation	状況 jyookyoo	street	通り toori	tax	税 zei
sleep	眠る nemuru	streetcar	路面電車 romen densha	tax included	税込の zeikomi no
sleeping medicine	睡眠薬 suimin-yaku	stubborn	頑固な ganko na	taxi stand	タクシー乗り場 takushii noriba
sleeve	袖 sode	study	勉強する benkyoo suru	teeth	歯 ha
slow	遅い osoi	stylish	おしゃれな oshare na	telephone	電話 denwa
small	小さい chiisai	subway	地下鉄 chikatetsu	telephone book	電話帳 denwa choo
smell (like something)	においがする nioi ga suru	suggest	提案する teian suru	telephone number	電話番号 denwa bangoo
smelly	くさい kusai	suit	似合う niau	tell, teach	教える oshieru
smoke a cigarette	たばこを吸う tabako o suu	sunburn	日焼け hiyake	temperature	気温 kion
smoking section	喫煙席 kitsuen seki	sunglasses	サングラス sangurasu	terrorism	テロ tero
soft	軟らかい yawarakai	sunny	晴れの hare no	theft	盗難 toonan
sold out	売切れの urikire no	sunrise	日の出 hinode	thermometer	体温計 taionkei

thick	厚い atsui	transformer	変圧器 hen-atsuki		
thief	ドロボウ doroboo	trash	ゴミ gomi	**W**	
thin, flat	薄い usui	trash can	ゴミ箱 gomi bako	waiting room	待合室 machiaishitsu
(be) thirsty	喉が渇いた nodo ga kawaita	trip, traveling	旅行 ryokoo	wake up	起きる okiru
three days from now	しあさって shiasatte	try a sample of food	試食する shishoku suru	wallet	財布 saifu
throat	喉 nodo	try on	試着する shichaku suru	warm, mild	暖かい atatakai
throw up	吐く haku	turn	曲がる magaru	waste	無駄遣い mudazukai
ticket	切符 kippu	**U**		watch	見る miru
ticket booth	チケット売り場 chiketto uriba	umbrella	傘 kasa	water	水 mizu
ticket gate	改札 kaisatsu	under construction	工事中 koojichuu	weak	弱い yowai
tight	きつい kitsui	underage	未成年 miseinen	weather	天気 tenki
time	時間 jikan	underground passage	地下道 chikadoo	weather report	天気予報 tenki yohoo
time difference	時差 jisa	understand	わかる wakaru	weekday	平日 heijitsu
time required	所要時間 shoyoo jikan	underwear	下着 shitagi	weekend	週末 shuumatsu
timetable	時刻表 jikokuhyoo	unusual	珍しい mezurashii	well	元気な genki na
(be) tired	疲れた tsukareta	used	中古の chuuko no	wide	広い hiroi
(buy food) to go	持ち帰る mochikaeru	**V**		with an ocean view	海の見える umi no mieru
toiletries	洗面用具 semmen yoogu	vacant	空きの aki no	withdraw (money)	下ろす orosu
toothache	歯痛 haita	vacant seat	空席 kuuseki	wonderful	すばらしい subarashii
toothbrush	歯ブラシ haburashi	vacuum	掃除機 soojiki	work	働く hataraku
toothpaste	歯磨き粉 hamigakiko	valid	有効な yuukoo na	(be) worried	心配だ shimpai da
touch	触る sawaru	valuables	貴重品 kichoohin	wound	傷 kizu
tourist attractions	観光地 kankoochi	vegetable	野菜 yasai	wring	しぼる shiboru
traffic accident	交通事故 kootsuu jiko	vending machine	自動販売機 jidoo hambaiki	wristwatch	腕時計 udedokei
traffic jam	交通渋滞 kootsuu juutai	vending stand	キオスク kiosuku	write	書く kaku
traffic sign	交通標識 kootsuu hyooshiki	victim	犠牲者 giseisha	wrong	間違った machigatta
train track	線路 senro	visit	訪ねる tazuneru	**X**	
				X-ray	レントゲン rentogen

Getting Proficient

143

絵を見て話せる
タビトモ会話

LIFE IN JAPAN
日本で暮らそう 英語[English] + 日本語[Japanese]

絵を見て話せる
タビトモ会話

<アジア>
①韓国
②中国
③香港
④台湾
⑤タイ
⑥バリ島
⑦ベトナム
⑧フィリピン
⑨カンボジア
⑩マレーシア
⑪インドネシア
⑫ネパール
⑬ソウル
⑭バンコク
⑮上海

<ヨーロッパ>
①イタリア
②ドイツ
③フランス
④スペイン
⑤ロシア
⑥フィンランド
⑦スウェーデン
⑧ポルトガル

<中近東>
①トルコ
②エジプト

<アメリカ>
②カナダ

<中南米>
①ペルー

<ビジネス>
ビジネス中国語

<JAPAN>
⑩LIFE IN JAPAN

続刊予定

インド
イギリス
オランダ
チェコ
アメリカ
ブラジル
メキシコ
ハワイ
オーストラリア

タビ会話
758390

初版印刷	2010年8月15日
初版発行	2010年9月1日 (Sep. 1, 2010, 1st edition)
編集人	百目鬼智子
発行人	竹浪　譲
発行所	JTBパブリッシング
印刷所	JTB印刷

●企画／編集　　　海外情報部
●編集協力　　　　長尾和夫／フォースター紀子
　　　　　　　　　（アルファ・プラス・カフェ）
　　　　　　　　　(財)英語教育協議会 (ELEC)
　　　　　　　　　／James Watt
●翻訳／校正　　　Ted Richards／Andy Boerger
　　　　　　　　　（アルファ・プラス・カフェ）
●表紙デザイン　　高多　愛 (Aleph Zero, inc.)
●本文デザイン　　Aleph Zero, inc.
●地図　　　　　　ジェイ・マップ
●イラスト　　　　浜野史子／霧生さなえ
●マンガ　　　　　ゼリービーンズ
●組版　　　　　　JTB印刷

●JTBパブリッシング
〒162-8446
東京都新宿区払方町25-5
編集：☎03-6888-7878
販売：☎03-6888-7893
広告：☎03-6888-7831
http://www.jtbpublishing.com/

●旅とおでかけ旬情報
http://rurubu.com/

JTBパブリッシング

禁無断転載・複製
©JTB Publishing 2010 Printed in Japan
104461　758390　ISBN978-4-533-07976-4